Maine Lighthouses

A Pictorial Guide

Maine Lighthouses

A Pictorial Guide

Courtney Thompson

Designed, edited and produced by
CatNap Publications
Brunswick, Maine

ISBN: 0-9651786-2-5
Library of Congress Catalog Number: 96-96249

Photography and text: Courtney Thompson
Maps and line graphics:
Wesley A. Shaw, Ripples Graphics
Mt. Desert, Me.

Color separations by N.S. Digital Technologies

Printed in Canada by
Quebecor Printing Atlantic
Saint John, New Brunswick
Canada

For purchase information please contact:
CatNap Publications
P.O. Box 172
Brunswick, ME 04011-0172

For my father. His forethought and love
made this project possible

 Table of Contents

Bold Coast

Downeast Coast

Mt. Desert Area

Eggemoggin Reach

Penobscot Bay

Midcoast

Kennebec River/Boothbay Area

Casco Bay/West Coast

Introduction

A lighthouse can be at once peaceful, lonely, beautiful, forlorn, silent, raucous, signaling both welcome and warning. Although often subject to harsh, unforgiving conditions, lighthouses also enjoy locations of breathtaking beauty. The benevolent appearance of the lighthouse brought about by clear skies and calm seas often is readily replaced with a presence of foreboding and loneliness as dense fog and rough seas cause the character of the lighthouse to change entirely. Lighthouses which host summer visitors, in winter become wonderfully deserted and peaceful; those which in summer offer a challenging, appealing destination for vacationing sailors, become isolated and lonely, facing winter's storms head on.

Primarily, however, a lighthouse represents stability and certainty; therein lies a strength of purpose which many find in them. The character of the sea constantly changes. So too the destination and inclination of the individual may alter. But the lighthouse provides a constant point of reference and assurance amidst changes. Although it's suggested that the technical function of the lighthouse is no longer needed for navigation, it is the intangible elements the lighthouse provides which cannot be replaced.

This book, then, is intended to offer a comprehensive guide to Maine lighthouses. What began as a personal goal to visit, document and photograph each light turned into a project of unexpected scope. While travelling the coast of Maine, I found books which included photographs, directions, technical/ historical information in varied combination. However, none of the available titles provided a complete compilation of the information: varied photographs, general information/history, directions and a small map of the immediate area. Therefore, my objective was the collection of these elements into one volume.

In order to visit, revisit and photograph the Maine lighthouses, I followed well-travelled routes, discovered many meandering back roads, explored peninsulas, coves and islands. I was able to experience the beauty of the Maine coast from three venues (land, sea, air); each added a new, extended dimension to my appreciation of the wonder of this coast. Moreover, the many people I met during this adventure were friendly, helpful, patient and cooperative; all were accommodating and understanding when the vagaries of coastal weather caused unexpected changes or improvisation in schedule, routes and plans.

An individual contribution to this effort must be acknowledged. Wes Shaw took me to see the lighthouses in the Mt. Desert area and beyond, some more than once. Since learning of my project and plans, he has provided hours of counsel and expertise in creating the maps included in this book. Additionally, Louise Shaw extended warm friendship and hospitality. Their guidance, support and encouragement contributed in large part to the completion of this project.

Finally, my thanks to all who helped me along the way, in whatever way.

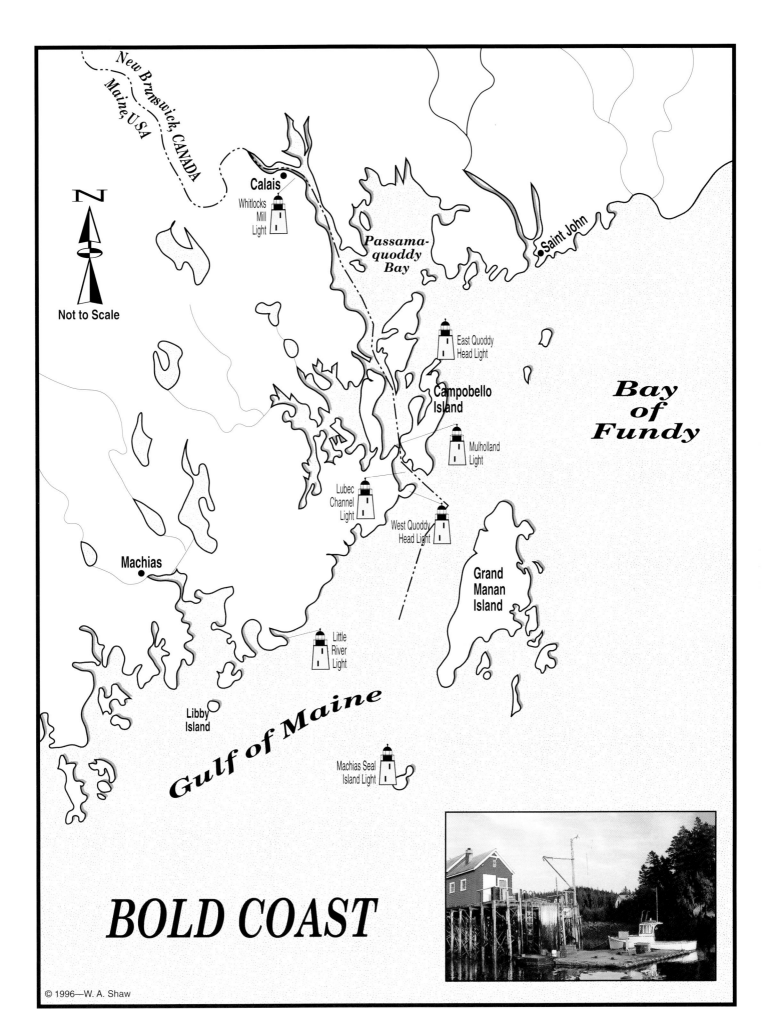

New Brunswick, CANADA

Maine, USA

N

Not to Scale

Calais

Whitlocks
Mill
Light

Passama-
quoddy
Bay

Saint John

East Quoddy
Head Light

Campobello
Island

Bay
of
Fundy

Mulholland
Light

Lubec
Channel
Light

West Quoddy
Head Light

Grand
Manan
Island

Machias

Little
River
Light

Libby
Island

Gulf of Maine

Machias Seal
Island Light

BOLD COAST

East Quoddy Light:

Located on the northern end of Campobello Island, New Brunswick, the light is maintained by the Canadian Coast Guard. The large red cross, typical of Canadian lights, is intended to make it easier to see against a snowy background. The light is also known as Head Harbour Light.

 Coast
Guard

Extreme
Hazard

Beach exposed only at low tide. Incoming tide rises 5 feet per hour, and may leave you stranded for 8 hours. Wading or swimming are extremely dangerous due to swift currents and cold water.

Proceed at your own risk.

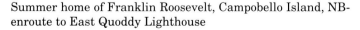

Summer home of Franklin Roosevelt, Campobello Island, NB-enroute to East Quoddy Lighthouse

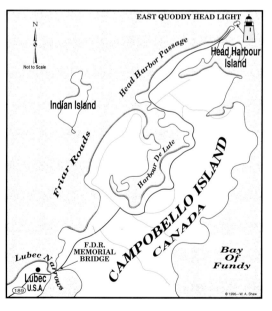

Directions: Cross into Canada at Lubec, Maine and continue approximately 2.5 miles past the customs station and Roosevelt Park. Turn right at a"Y" intersection, NB 774North. Continue on this road for about seven miles through Wilson's Beach to Head Harbour and the light. The Lighthouse Rd. becomes a dirt road shortly before ending at the parking area.

There are trails around the area, including series of iron rail stairways which make the light accessible directly at low tide only. A sign warns of rapidly changing tides and weather conditions; there is about a two-hour period to cross and return from the light without being stranded on the island for six to eight hours.

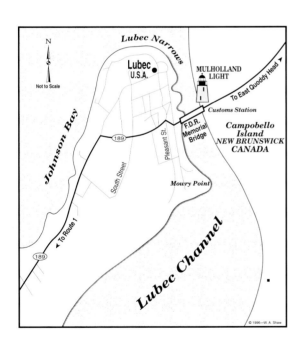

Directions: Cross over to New Brunswick, Canada at Lubec, Maine, taking the first left after the customs station, just opposite the welcome/information center. The road leads down a hill, then bears right; a small park and the light are just to the left.

Mulholland Light:

On the east side of Lubec Channel on Campobello Island, the light is easily seen from the Maine side of the channel and is easily accessible from the Canadian side.Mulholland is not a functioning light.

"Mulholland Point Lighthouse
Erected 1885
Donated to
Roosevelt Campobello International Park
December 4, 1985"

Whitlock's Mill Light:

The lighthouse is located on the south bank of the St. Croix River at Calais, Maine and is the northernmost light. The light was automated in 1968 and the keeper's house is now privately owned.

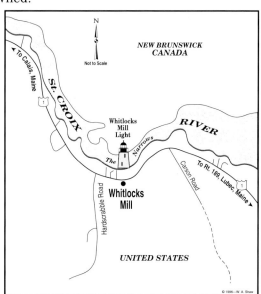

Directions: The light can be located by taking U.S. Route 1 from Whiting, through Red Beach to the Taylor Furniture Store, just south of Calais. **Turn around** and count four driveways **back on the left** from the store (to the south). A narrow, dirt road leads to the light and private residence; the area is not a public park. The light also can be seen in the distance from a roadside park area off Route 1, about five miles north from the entrance to the St. Croix Island International Historic Site.

Lubec Channel Light:

Built in 1890, this light is on the west side of the Lubec Channel at Lubec, Maine. It is often referred to as the "Spark Plug." In 1989 the Coast Guard announced plans to abandon the tower, moving the optic and lantern to a shore location, rather than afford the estimated $1 million in needed repairs. However, efforts by concerned Lubec residents and the Maine Historic Preservation Commission enabled the light to be restored at a cost of about $700,000.

Directions: Turn off U.S. Route 1 at Whiting, onto ME 189 to Lubec. Continue about four miles, then turn right onto South Lubec/Boot Cove Road (marked with a "Quoddy Head State Park" sign). The Lubec Channel light can be seen to the left at about 1/3 to 1/2 mile; it can also be seen from ME 189 crossing into Canada. Additionally, there are tour boats out of Lubec which afford closer views of this light.

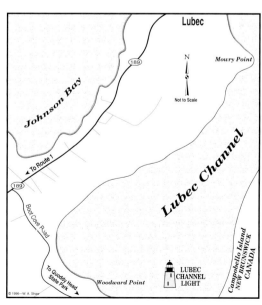

West Quoddy Light:

Located on the easternmost point in the continental United States, the red and white striped light marks the southwest entrance to Quoddy Channel. The light was originally built in 1807 under orders of Thomas Jefferson, then rebuilt in 1858. The white flashing light is visible for 18 miles. Before installation of a steam whistle in 1869, the keeper was required to strike a bell by hand in foggy weather and, for his trouble, was allotted an extra $60 annually. The "west" in West Quoddy Head refers to its location west of East Quoddy Head Light in nearby New Brunswick, Canada.

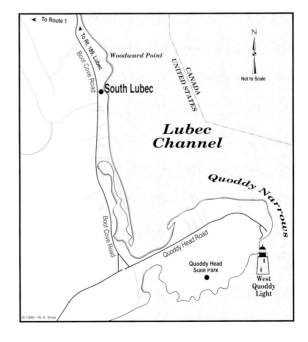

Directions: From U.S. Route 1 at Whiting, Maine turn onto ME 189 and continue for about four miles. Turn right onto South Lubec/Boot Cove Road (marked with a "Quoddy Head State Park" sign) and continue to a fork in the road, again marked with "Quoddy Head State Park". Bear left and continue on to the park and light station. At the entrance to the station turn right onto the road leading to the parking area. A short trail to the left leads to the light; other trails to the right offer views of the light, cliffs and islands.

Little River Light:

The light, built originally in 1847 and rebuilt in 1876, is located at the mouth of Little River at the entrance to Cutler Harbor. In addition to marking the entrance to the harbor, this lighthouse was intended as an intermediate mark between West Quoddy Head to the north and Machias Seal Island to the southeast but is now inactive. On the seaward side of a wooded, offshore island, this lighthouse can be seen only by boat or from the air. Cutler is a small fishing village with one of the prettiest harbors in Maine.

Directions: From U.S. Route 1 at East Machias, turn south onto RT 191. Follow that road into Cutler Harbor where charter arrangements may be made.

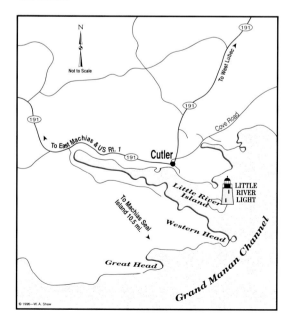

Machias Seal Island Light:

Twelve miles off the coast from Cutler, Maine, this light station is maintained by the Canadian government although it is in Maine waters. Canadian lightkeepers man the light due to a question of sovereignty, with both Canada and the United States claiming the two islands and surrounding waters. The island is home to a large puffin colony and other sea birds, carefully protected by the Canadian Wildlife Service. Charter trips to view the light and the puffins are available from Cutler and Jonesport .

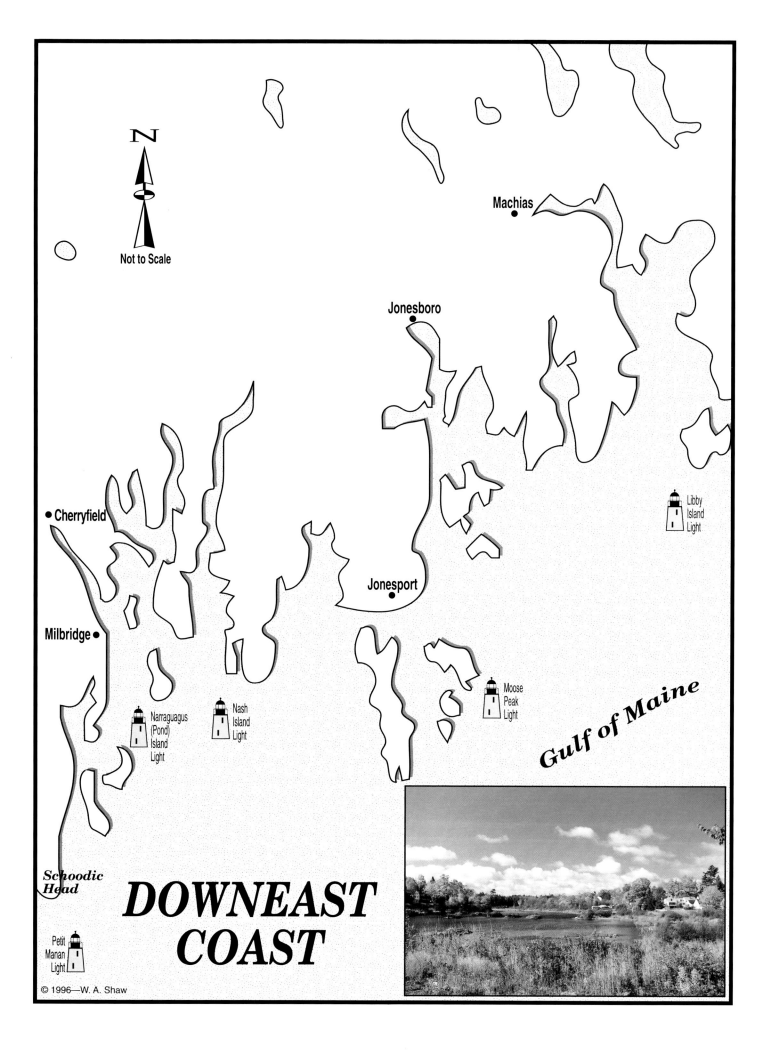

N

Not to Scale

Machias

Jonesboro

Cherryfield

Libby
Island
Light

Jonesport

Milbridge

Moose
Peak
Light

Narraguagus
(Pond)
Island
Light

Nash
Island
Light

Gulf of Maine

Schoodic
Head

**DOWNEAST
COAST**

Petit
Manan
Light

Libby Island Light:

On the southern tip of the island, the light marks the southern entrance to Machias Bay and was known for many years as Machias Light. The light was built originally in 1817, rebuilt in 1824 and is the easternmost lighthouse in the United States. Heavy fogs often engulf this area; the most notable of vessels wrecked in the area was the schooner *Caledonia*, 1878, out of Nova Scotia.

Moose Peak Light:

This light is located on the east side of Mistake Island, to the east of Great Wass Island, south of Jonesport. Built in 1827 and rebuilt in 1887, the light can be seen for 25 miles as it guards one of the foggiest areas of the coast. Although on a perfectly clear day, the light can be seen in the distance from Great Wass Island, it is best viewed from the air or by boat.

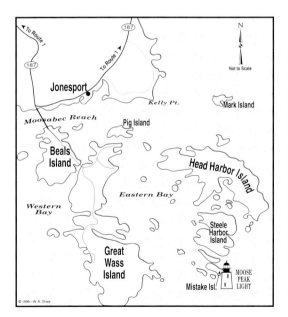

Directions: In Jonesport at the "Bridge Street" and " Beal's Island" signs turn off ME 187 onto the bridge to Beal's Island. On the island, turn left and continue on Great Wass Road across Beal's Island to the road's end on Great Wass Island. Walk to the top of the rocky knoll or walk along the shore to the point; Moose Peak light can be seen in the distance, to the east, in the V-shaped part of the island.

Nash Island Light:

The lighthouse, built in 1838 and rebuilt in 1873, is located on the east side entrance to Pleasant Bay near South Addison. Automated in 1958 and later discontinued and replaced by a lighted buoy in 1981, all that remains of the station is the light tower. The remains of the foundation(s) of the keeper's house and outbuildings are still visible; the tower is in disrepair. However, this station was one of the few where the children of lighthouse keepers attended school on the island for the earlier grades. This light can be reached only by air or by boat.

Petit Manan Light:

Established in 1817 and rebuilt of granite in 1855, this is the second tallest lighthouse in Maine, standing 123 feet above mean high water (the tower is 119 feet high). The light is located on the east point of Petit Manan Island, 2.5 miles off Petit Manan Point in South Milbridge. The station also has a fog signal to warn of a nearby reef; the location is one of the foggiest along the East Coast, engulfed in fog about 20% of the year.

The process of rebuilding the light in 1855 was twofold . The granite was first cut and assembled at a quarry in Trenton, Maine. Numbered stones were dismantled and brought to the island by boat for reassembly. Petit Manan Island is now managed by the U.S. Fish & Wildlife Service, with the light (automated in 1972) under Coast Guard jurisdiction and assistance from the Maine Historic Preservation Commission in restoration/repair of the tower. A second order lens, previously in the tower, is displayed at the Shore Village Museum in Rockland, Maine.

The light and island are best photographed by air or boat. However, on clear days this light can be seen in the distance from the shore south of Milbridge.

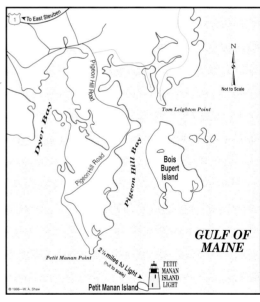

Directions: On U.S. Route 1, between Steuben and Milbridge, turn south onto Pigeon Hill Rd (marked). The turn is approximately three miles **west** of the intersection of US 1 and US 1A in Milbridge and three miles **east** of the Unionville & Steuben Rd. intersection. Continue on Pigeon Hill Rd. to the Chitman Point area (approximately 5.5-6.0 miles) to the fisherman's coop. Petit Manan can be seen in the distance. Continuing further south about 0.5 mile brings you to the Petit Manan National Wildlife Refuge . There is a parking lot straight ahead; just south of the parking lot is the beginning of a five-mile Shore Trail. The first two miles of the trail lead to the eastern side of Petit Manan Point peninsula and good, distant views of the light.

Narraguagus (Pond) Island Light:

Called Pond Island Light by people in the area, the lighthouse is located southeast of Milbridge, Maine on a rock ledge on the seaward side of Pond Island in Narraguagus Bay. The light was built in 1853 and the present keeper's house built in 1875. After deactivation of the light in 1934, Pond Island became a posh resort with inn and golf course. Only the privately-owned light station now remains. As with Nash Island the light can be seen only from the air or by boat.

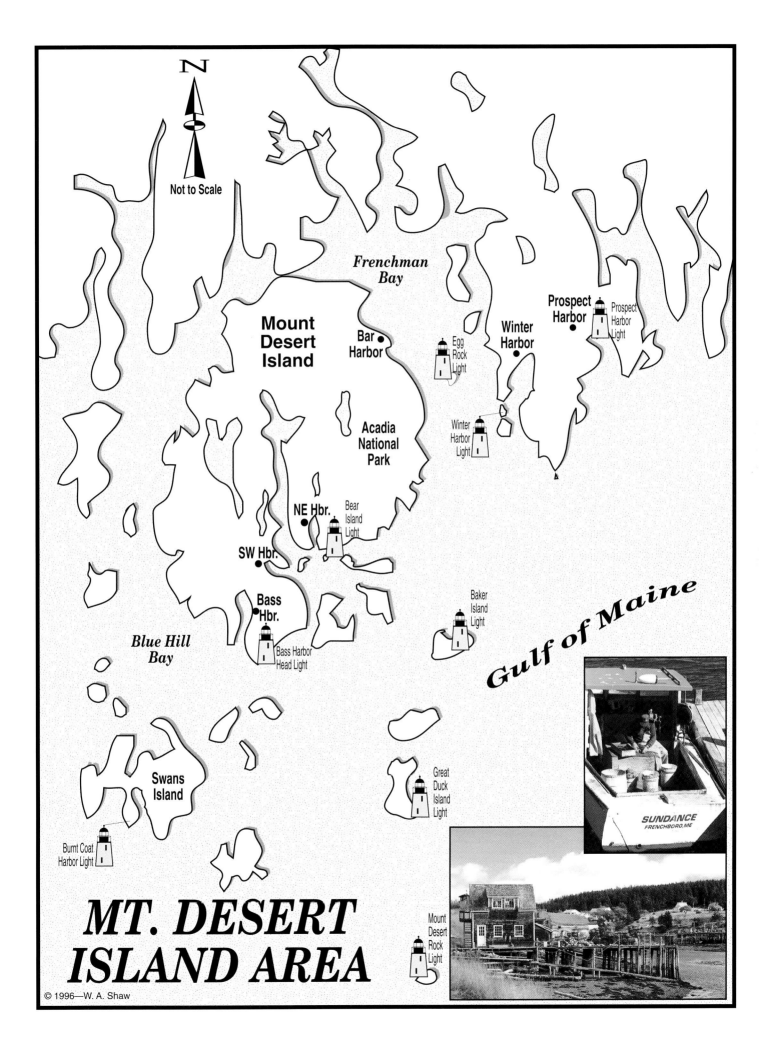

N

Not to Scale

Frenchman
Bay

Mount
Desert
Island

Bar
Harbor

Egg
Rock
Light

Winter
Harbor

Prospect
Harbor

Prospect
Harbor
Light

Acadia
National
Park

Winter
Harbor
Light

NE Hbr.

Bear
Island
Light

SW Hbr.

Baker
Island
Light

Gulf of Maine

Bass
Hbr.

Blue Hill
Bay

Bass Harbor
Head Light

SUNDANCE
FRENCHBORO, ME

Swans
Island

Great
Duck
Island
Light

Burnt Coat
Harbor Light

MT. DESERT
ISLAND AREA

Mount
Desert
Rock
Light

Winter Harbor (Mark Island) Light:

This light, built in 1856, is on Mark Island across Frenchman Bay from Bar Harbor. Privately owned since 1934, the light is no longer functioning. Although best photographed from the water or air, the lighthouse can be seen from the Schoodic Peninsula section of Acadia National Park.

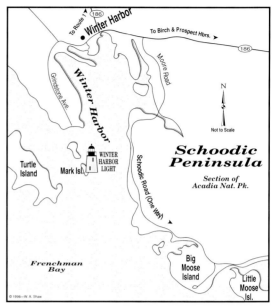

Directions: From U.S. Route 1, turn south onto ME 186 at West Gouldsboro, toward Schoodic Point. Turn off ME 186 at the marked road leading to Acadia National Park, Schoodic Peninsula (between Birch Harbor and Winter Harbor). The park's perimeter road is a one-way loop and the lighthouse/island can be seen from that road. Excursion and tour boats from Bar Harbor offer closer views for better photography.

Prospect Harbor Light:

On the east side of the inner harbor, the lighthouse built in 1850 and rebuilt in 1891, is now part of an active military base (U.S. Navy special communications station). The Lighthouse Board deactivated the light in 1859 but reactivated it in 1870; the light was automated in 1934. The lighthouse can be easily photographed from the Prospect Harbor area.

Directions: From U.S. Route 1, take either ME 186 or 195 to Prospect Harbor. Turn at the sign to Corea at the intersection of these two routes. FR 605 (Lighthouse Point Road) is about 0.2 mile—ME 195 bears left to Corea, but continue straight on FR 605 to the restricted U.S. Navy communications station. The light is easily photographed from the shoreline. Alternatively, across the harbor the light can be seen and photographed from the grounds of the Stinson Canning Company (on ME 186 entering Prospect Harbor) or from a turnout on the shoulder of ME 186, just north of the canning company.

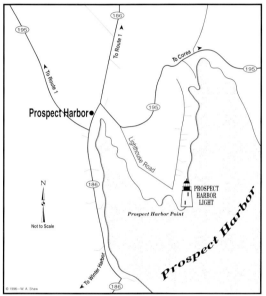

Egg Rock Light:

The light, built in 1875, sits atop the keeper's house to conserve space, as the lighthouse is built on a small exposed island, marking the entrance to upper Frenchman Bay. In 1976 the light was automated and the lantern room removed. The 4th order Fresnel (prism type) lens was replaced with aero beacons. This caused a change in appearance not to the liking of most; in 1986 the tower was refitted with an octagonal aluminum lantern and railing around the lantern deck perimeter in order to improve appearance. Nevertheless, this light has become known as the most homely on the Maine coast.

Most excursion boats out of Bar Harbor pass this light; it also is visible from many scenic overlooks in Acadia National Park.

Directions: The Loop Road in Acadia National park offers distant views of this light from several scenic overlooks on the eastern side of the park. For a closer view and photographs, several tour/whale watching boats out of Bar Harbor pass this lighthouse.

33

Great Duck Island Light:

Located about six miles southeast of Bass Harbor, the light was built in 1890 at the direction of President Benjamin Harrison. Large flocks of ducks arrived at a pond on the island each spring to raise their young, hence the name "Great Duck". The island, although remote, once had a one-teacher school for all grades built in 1904; one keeper who served from 1902-1912 had 16 children who attended along with the children of two other keepers.

The lighthouse was intended to direct vessels into Bass Harbor or Southwest Harbor, both offering safe refuge in storms. A small burial ground behind the lighthouse marks the grave of two shipwrecked mariners found frozen to death in each other's arms.

In 1984 the Maine Chapter of the Nature Conservancy purchased the privately owned island. The light was automated in 1986 and the Coast Guard retained jurisdiction over the light station until 1992, at which time the Conservancy gained full control of the station. The keeper's house is used as a base for ecological research & study of seabirds. Major repairs to the tower were undertaken in 1994 and completed in the summer of 1995.

Directions: The light may be seen only from the air or by boat. Whale watching trips from Bar Harbor generally head in the direction of this lighthouse but the course often changes according to location of the whales.

Major work was done on the lighthouse during the fall of 1994 and summer of 1995. Initial plans were to leave the tower unpainted, but mariners reported that it too easily blended into the adjacent outbuildings and therefore was not clearly visible. The tower was repainted white in the fall of 1995.

Mt. Desert Rock Light:

Clearly one of the most isolated light-houses along the Maine coast, this light was built in 1830 on the tiny island, approximately 600 yards long and 200 yards wide, some 25 nautical miles south of Mt. Desert Island. The tower was replaced in 1847; the light was automated in 1977 and is solar powered.

Even in relatively mild storms waves wash over the island. An 1842 report by Maine's Superintendent of Lighthouses noted that a storm relocated a 57-ton granite boulder on the island; the report also mentioned that another storm moved a 75-ton boulder some 60 feet. Because the island has no topsoil, gardening was a challenge. Each spring keepers would bring barrels and bags of soil to establish vegetable and flower gardens. And each fall and winter the results of those efforts would be washed away by the sea.

During the summer months the lighthouse has been used as an observation post by marine scientists from the College of the Atlantic's Allied Whale while study-ing the activities of whales in the area.

Directions: The light can be seen only by boat or by air. Whale-watching trips usually head to feeding grounds in the Mt. Desert Rock area, so the lighthouse may be seen from one of these excursions. However, because the route is determined by location of the whales, close views of the light cannot always be guaranteed. The trip to the light is approximately 1.5-2 hours each way and weather can often preclude good viewing and photography.

Baker Island Light:

At the southwest entrance to Frenchman Bay, this light is located on a 123-acre wooded island which is now part of Acadia National Park. The light was originally built in 1828 under order of President John Quincy Adams, then rebuilt in 1855 and automated in 1966. It is now solar powered. Primarily a harbor entrance light, it marks the shoals around the Cranberry Isles. The light's first keeper was long-time island resident William Gilley who remained on the island 21 years to attend the light.

The Coast Guard in 1991 planned to deactivate the light, allowing that trees were obscuring the light. The Friends of Acadia attempted to prevent that action by getting the National Park Service to trim the trees. However, as of fall 1995, the trees are still hiding the light from clear view from the water.

The light is best seen from the air or by a boat trip to the island which takes you ashore to explore the island and visit the lighthouse.

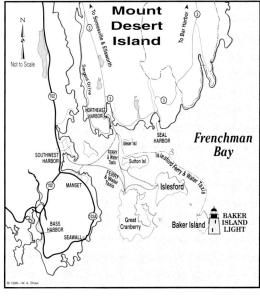

Directions: From ME 3 or 233 (Eagle Lake Road) in Mt. Desert, take ME 198 south to Northeast Harbor. Turn left off ME 198 in Northeast Harbor at Harbor Drive (sign indicates "marina"). The *Islesford Ferry,* docked at Northeast Harbor Marina, offers trips to the island. A naturalist (sponsored by Acadia National Park) accompanies visitors and leads a walk which includes a visit to the lighthouse. Also by custom charter.

Bear Island Light:

The entrance to Northeast Harbor on Mt. Desert Island was marked by this light, built in 1839 and rebuilt in 1889. In 1982 the light station was deactivated and replaced by offshore lighted buoys and the property incorporated into Acadia National Park in 1987. The light was reestablished as a private aid to navigation in 1989. Since 1991 the station has been leased by the National Park Service to a private owner in exchange for specified repairs to the buildings. The improvements & renovations have, in my view, made this lighthouse one of the most beautiful and appealing on the Maine coast.

The light may be seen easily by boat; the mail boat/ferry to Cranberry Isles out of Northeast Harbor operates year 'round and offers good views. The ferry from Southwest Harbor to Cranberry Isles (June- September) also passes the lighthouse as do tour boats out of Bar Harbor during July and August. Charter boasts from Northeast Harbor also pass this light.

Directions: The ferries/mailboat to Cranberry Isles pass this lighthouse.

To Northeast Harbor:From ME 3 or 233 (Eagle Lake Road), take ME 198 south to Northeast Harbor. Turn left off ME 198 in Northeast Harbor at Harbor Drive (sign indicates "marina"). Ferry/mailboat:*Sea Queen, Double B*

To Southwest Harbor: Take ME 3 or ME 233 to ME 198/102--signs clearly indicate directions. Continue on RT. 102 south to Southwest Harbor--turn left in town at the sign to upper town dock. Ferry: *Island Queen.*

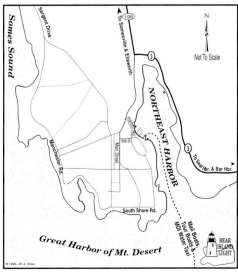

39

Bass Harbor Head Light:

One of the most photographed in Maine, this lighthouse is located on the southwest point of Mt. Desert, marking the entrance of Blue Hill Bay and Bass Harbor. Because the harbor offered refuge from easterly gales, the light was built in 1858 as a guide to ships seeking shelter. The keeper's house is now a Coast Guard family residence. Although the station is easily accessible by car, it is much more impressive when viewed from the water.

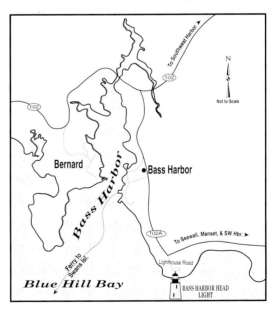

Directions: Follow RT 3 from Ellsworth to ME 198; turn south onto ME 102 and continue through Bass Harbor to the Coast Guard Bass Harbor Head Station entrance. There are trails east of the parking area which lead down to large granite boulders at the shore; best views/photographs of the light from land are taken from these rocks.

From the water: Follow "Swans Island Ferry" signs through Bass Harbor, turning right onto Swans Island Road and the ferry landing. The ferry operates year round. This light is easily incorporated into most custom boat or air charter lighthouse routes.

41

Burnt Coat Harbor Light (Hockamock Head):

A set of range lights originally was built on the southwest tip of Swans Island in 1872. The lights were built a distance apart, with the rear light at higher elevation; a safe channel was indicated when the lights lined up. However, after complaints that the two lights caused confusion on approaching the harbor (coupled with an increase in number of shipwrecks), the Lighthouse Board removed the smaller front range light in 1885.

In 1994 the Coast Guard turned the property over to the Town of Swans Island; plans were to develop a public park at the station. Swans Island can be reached by car ferry from Bass Harbor. From the ferry landing it is about five miles to the light.

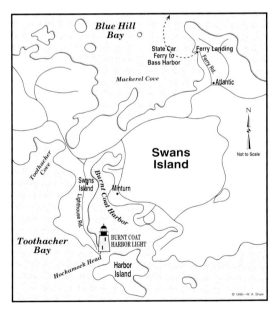

Directions: Follow "Swans Island Ferry" signs, taking ME 102 into Bass Harbor, then turn right to the ferry landing. On the island, turn right at the ferry landing, then right again at the next intersection. Continue southeast on this main road about one mile, then bear left at the fork past the Minturn turnoff into the village of Swans Island. The road ends, bear left onto a narrow path to a parking area at the lighthouse. A car is unnecessary as the route is an easy bicycle trip.

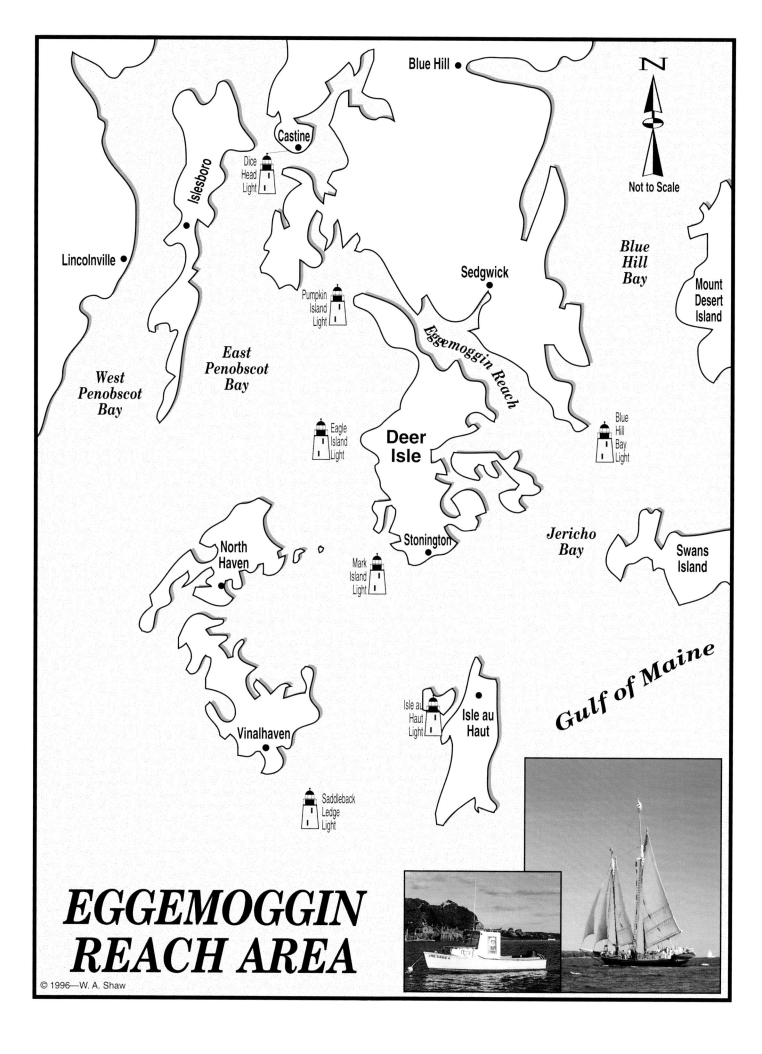

Blue Hill •

N

Not to Scale

Castine •

Dice
Head
Light

Islesboro

Lincolnville •

Sedgwick •

*Blue
Hill
Bay*

Mount
Desert
Island

Pumpkin
Island
Light

Eggemoggin Reach

*East
Penobscot
Bay*

*West
Penobscot
Bay*

Eagle
Island
Light

**Deer
Isle**

Blue
Hill
Bay
Light

Stonington

*Jericho
Bay*

Swans
Island

North
Haven

Mark
Island
Light

Isle au
Haut
Light

Isle au
Haut

Gulf of Maine

Vinalhaven

Saddleback
Ledge
Light

EGGEMOGGIN
REACH AREA

Saddleback Ledge Light:

Built in 1839 on a small ledge of rock between Isle au Haut and Vinalhaven, this lighthouse is among the most remote on the Maine coast. The island has no soil and, when manned, the light had the dubious distinction of being the most difficult on which to make a landing. Keepers brought dirt to the island in an effort to grow vegetables, but their work was faithfully taken away each year by winter storms. The light was automated in the 1960s and can be photographed only by air or boat.

Isle au Haut Light:

Named "high island" by Samuel de Champlain in 1604, this island is part of Acadia National Park, six miles south of Stonington, Maine. The lighthouse, built in 1907, is located on Robinson Point about 0.8 mile from the town landing, over-looking the Isle au Haut Thorofare and Kimball Island. When automated in 1934 the property (except the tower) was sold at auction. The keeper's house is now operated as a bed and breakfast and is on the National Register of Historic Places.

Ferry and mail boat service are available to the island; scenic cruises of the island region also afford views of the lighthouse.

Directions: To Stonington: Take U.S. Route 1 to Orland, turning right at the sign to Castine/Deer Isle. Follow RT 175 through Penobscot, then RT 175/ 15 to Deer Isle into Stonington. On Main Street at Atlantic Avenue turn left to the Atlantic Avenue Dock. Parking is metered and day-long/ overnight spaces are limited;ask at the dock area before parking long term.

From the island town landing: Turn right onto the main road and walk about 3/4 mile; bear right onto a narrow path (marked with a "Keeper's House" sign). The lighthouse is about 0.5 mile ahead. Maps of the island are available in Stonington or on the mailboat.

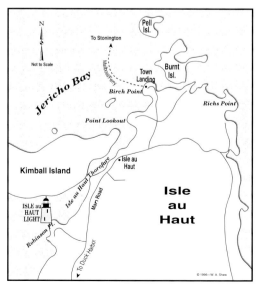

Deer Island Thorofare/Mark Island Light:

On the west end of Mark Island in Penobscot Bay, this light was built in 1857 and guards the western approach to the Deer Island Thorofare. The keeper's house was demolished when the light was automated; today only the square tower and entryway remain. Although the light can be seen in the distance with binoculars from Stonington and points along Route 15, it is best photographed by boat or air.

Blue Hill Bay Light:

This lighthouse was constructed in 1856-57 on Green Island in Blue Hill Bay. Because the island is so flat, its dimensions change drastically with the tide. Flye Island is nearby and can be reached at low tide over a sand and rock bar. The station is now inactive and a privately owned home; the active light operates from a skeleton tower at the south end of the property. Green Island is a few miles north of Swans Island and can be seen only by boat or air.

The island and light at high tide...

.....and at low tide.

Pumpkin Island Light:

This light is located at the northern end of Eggemoggin Reach, just off Little Deer Island on what was once called Tent Island. Built in 1854 and automated in 1930, the light is no longer operational and has been privately owned since 1934. Although it is possible to view and photograph the light from land, it is best seen by boat or air.

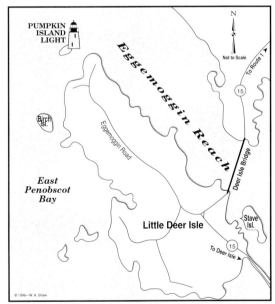

Directions: From U.S. Route 1 at Orland, turn south toward Castine (sign indicates Castine/Deer Isle) onto ME 175. Follow ME 175/15 south through Penobscot and Sargentville. Turn right to Little Deer Isle, continue across the Deer Island suspension bridge. Bear right at the end of the bridge (RT 15 turns left) onto Eggemoggin Road. Continue 2.6 miles to the road's end at a fishing pier near the Eggemoggin Inn. Pumpkin Island can be seen just off shore.

Eagle Island Light:

The lighthouse on 260-acre Eagle Island in Penobscot Bay, between Deer Isle and North Haven, was first built in 1839 then rebuilt in 1858. On the northeast end of the island, the light is difficult to see clearly from the water, especially when leaves on trees preclude an unobstructed view.

After automating the light in 1959, the Coast Guard in 1963 burned the keeper's house and demolished all other structures save the bell tower and light and removed all fixtures. When attempting to move the fogbell downhill to the shore, the bell slipped and was sent bouncing down over the cliff into the ocean. An unexpecting lobsterman came upon the bell sometime later, retrieved it and sold it to photographer Eliot Porter.

The light can only be viewed by boat or air.

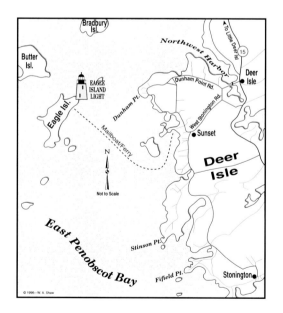

Via mailboat out of Sunset, Maine. Take RT 15 into Deer Isle and turn right at the post office (marked with a "Sunset" sign), bear right again at Pressey Village Road (0.5mile), then left onto Dunham Point Road. Continue on to Sylvester Cove (about 3.2 miles from the post office).

Dice Head Light:

Castine is a beautiful village whose quiet, historic elegance belies its eventful,vivid past. The town, located at the entrance to the Penobscot River, was initially settled as a trading post by the Pilgrims of Plymouth and later named after the Baron de St.Castine who took over the town in 1676. Because of its strategic location, Castine was variously occupied by the British, French and Dutch. In 1779, during the American Revolution, an entire American fleet was lost in the course of attempting to recapture Castine from the British; the ill-fated effort was led by Dudley Saltonstall with assistance from Paul Revere. Maine Maritime Academy also is located in Castine.

The lighthouse was built in 1829, then rebuilt in 1858 with the keeper's house again rebuilt in 1937. It is no longer a functioning light. The active light operates from a skeleton tower at the water's edge. After deactivation the station and eventually the entire property (including tower) became property of the Town of Castine. The keeper's house is rented with the income used for maintenance of the house. The lighthouse is easily accessible from the village.

(Continued, following page)

Dice Head Light

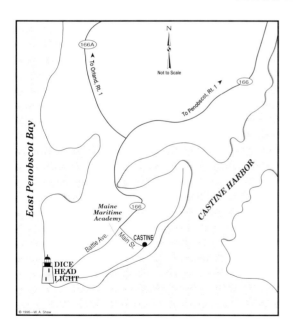

Directions: From U.S. Route 1 at Orland, take routes 175 and 166 to Castine. Continue one mile past Fort George and Maine Maritime Academy on Battle Avenue to the road's end. There is a public (marked) path to the left by the garage.

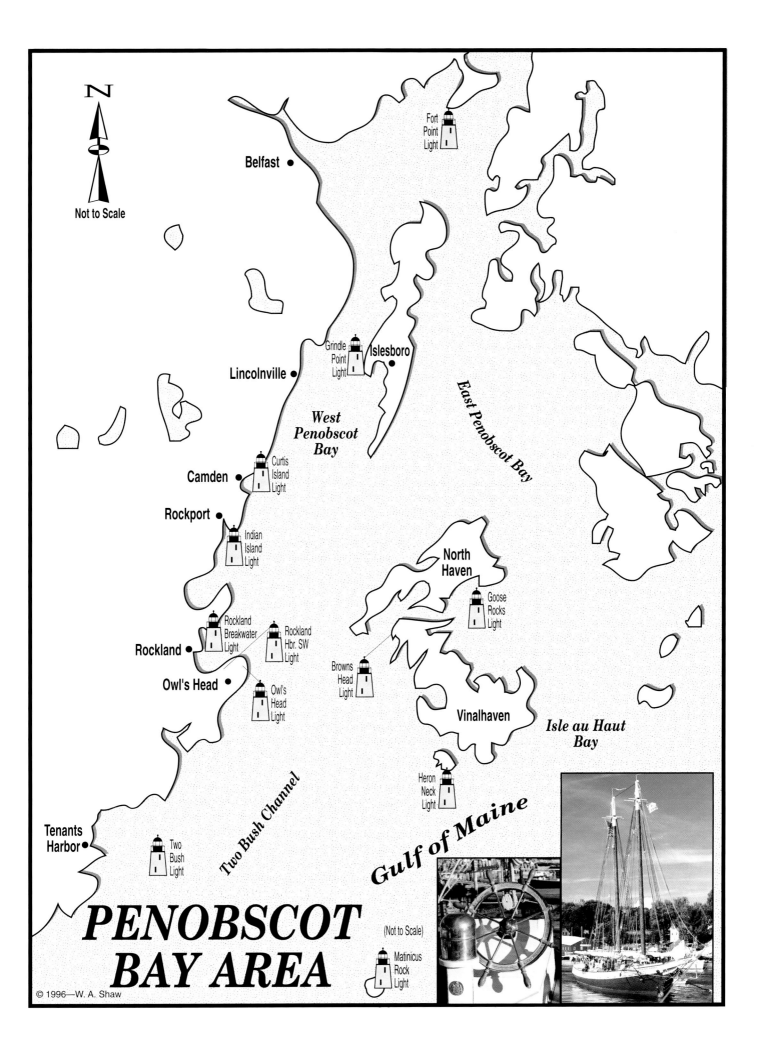

N

Not to Scale

Belfast •

Fort Point Light

Grindle Point Light
Islesboro •

Lincolnville •

West Penobscot Bay

East Penobscot Bay

Camden •
Curtis Island Light

Rockport •

Indian Island Light

North Haven

Goose Rocks Light

Rockland Breakwater Light
Rockland Hbr. SW Light

Rockland •

Browns Head Light

Owl's Head •
Owl's Head Light

Isle au Haut Bay

Vinalhaven

Heron Neck Light

Two Bush Channel

Gulf of Maine

Tenants Harbor •
Two Bush Light

(Not to Scale)

Matinicus Rock Light

PENOBSCOT BAY AREA

Fort Point Light:

President Andrew Jackson ordered this light built in 1836 on the west side of the mouth of the Penobscot River; it was rebuilt in 1857 and automated in 1988. The bell tower, one of the last of its type remaining, is listed in the National Register of Historic Places. Fort Point was the site of British-built Fort Pownall and the foundations of the fort may be seen near the light station. The park and lighthouse are easily accessible from Stockton Springs.

Directions: From U.S. Route 1 at Stockton Springs, take the turn marked "Stockton Springs". Continue about 0.5 mile through the small town and follow the Fort Point State Park sign, turning right onto East Cape Road. Follow that road to the park entrance; the park road is clearly marked and leads to a small parking area near the lighthouse. If the entrance gate is closed, park just outside and walk into the park about 0.75 mile to the lighthouse.

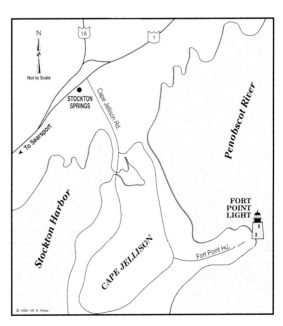

Grindle Point Light:

The lighthouse is located on the north side of the entrance to Gilkey Harbor and is named after Francis Grindle who originally owned the three-acre property on Islesboro on which the light station was built in 1851. Moreover, Mr. Grindle later was appointed the light's second keeper in April,1853. Rebuilt in 1874 after succumbing to the elements, the light was deactivated and sold to the Village of Islesboro in 1934. Fifty-three years later, in 1987, the light was recommissioned and converted to solar power. The Islesboro Sailor's Memorial Museum is now located in the keeper's house and the fogbell on the south side of the light tower is on loan from the Shore Village Museum in Rockland, Maine.

Although distantly visible from the mainland, the light is reached easily by taking the auto ferry from Lincolnville to Islesboro. The three-mile crossing takes 20 minutes; the lighthouse is at the ferry landing.

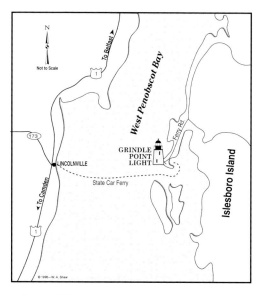

Directions: U.S. Route 1 to Lincolnville (north from Camden,south from Belfast). Follow signs to Islesboro Ferry. There is parking adjacent to the ferry landing.

58

Goose Rocks Light:

This light, which sits on a ledge in the middle of the Fox Island Thorofare marking the eastern entrance, is another caisson-type ("spark plug") lighthouse (also Lubec Channel, Spring Point Ledge). Built in 1890, the light is located between Vinalhaven and North Haven Islands; it was automated in 1963 and is solar powered.

Although a distant view is possible from Calderwood Point on Vinalhaven, the light is best photographed by boat or air. (See map with Browns Head Light, p.63)

Curtis Island Light:

Built in 1836, this light marks the south side
entrance to Camden Harbor. In the early 1600s
Captain John Smith arrived in Camden Harbor; on
the voyage with him was a black cook who, upon
seeing the small island in the harbor, allowed that
if he could have any place in the world, that island
would be the place. Captain Smith then declared
the cook to be the owner of the island, whereupon
it became "Negro Island".

The five-acre island was later owned by and named
after Cyrus Curtis, publisher of the *Saturday
Evening Post*. After automation in 1972 the lighthouse was deeded to the Town of Camden and is
now operated as a public park accessible by private
boat or water taxi. The keeper's house is rented in
the summer months.

Although there are several locations along the shore
offering distant views of this light, it is best seen
and photographed by boat or air. Any of the sight-
seeing or windjammer cruises departing from the Camden Harbor public landing will pass immediately in front of the lighthouse and afford excellent views. A trip on the *Betselma* offers particularly
good close-up views of the Curtis and Indian Island Lights during a one-hour cruise; the two-hour
cruise continues to Islesboro to view the Grindle Point light. Ticket tables for all cruises are at the
boardwalk at the public landing.

Directions: U.S. Route 1 to Camden. Turn onto Bayview Street, then left to the town wharf. Arrangements may be made to go to Curtis Island for the day or for a few hours to enjoy the park. The light also may be seen well in winter through the trees further up Bayview Street; the drives are private property and there is no access to the shorefront.

 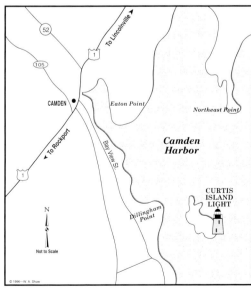

Browns Head Light:

The eastern end of the Fox Island Thorofare is marked by this light on the northwest point of Vinalhaven Island. Originally built in 1832, the light was replaced in 1857. For no apparent reason, the Coast Guard burned the fogbell tower when the crew was removed after automation in 1987. The Town of Vinalhaven then acquired the station buildings and grounds; the keeper's house is now rented.

Auto and passenger ferry service to Vinalhaven is available out of Rockland, Maine throughout the year. A vehicle reservation is mandatory to ensure a one-day round trip. The light can also be photographed by boat from the Fox Island Thorofare.

Fox Island Thorofare off Vinalhaven Island. Brown's Head and Goose Rocks Lighthouse are both seen from the Thorofare.

Directions: Take the ferry from Rockland to Vinalhaven. Coming off the ferry, turn right and follow Main and High Streets to North Haven Road. Turn right and continue for about six miles;be careful to keep track of mileage as there are no street signs or markers to the light. Look for a group of mailboxes at the intersection with a dirt road (Crockett River Road); turn left onto that road, then right at the second dirt road to the right. Pass a small cemetery on the right. There is a small parking area at the light.

Additionally, the Goose Rocks Lighthouse can be seen in the distance from Calderwood Point on Calderwood Neck. The road is unimproved; hiking to the point, rather than driving, is recommended.

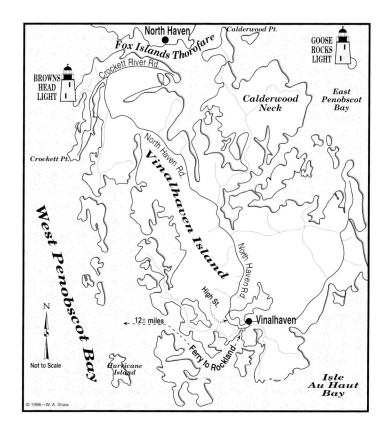

Heron Neck Light:

On the southern tip of Green Island, just southwest of Carver's Harbor on Vinalhaven, this light, built in 1854, marks the east entrance to Hurricane Sound. A fire in 1989 nearly destroyed the keeper's house; the light and tower were not damaged. Announcement by the Coast Guard in 1990 that there were no plans to rebuild the keeper's dwelling resulted in national publicity and offers to lease the station and restore the house.

Subsequently, the Coast Guard, lighthouse preservationists and historic preservation commission(s) became entangled in a battle of conflicting opinions/intents/interpretations, each claiming to offer the best course of action but at cross purposes. During a temporary halt in the feuding, the Island Institute of Rockland, Maine announced in 1993 that it was prepared to lease the light station's property, the house and outbuildings. The restoration is still in process.

The lighthouse is located on a sharply defined rock ledge on the island and may be viewed only by boat or air. Outward Bound's Hurricane Island is "next door".

Windjammer cruises out of Camden, Rockport and/or Rockland often pass this lighthouse and offer an opportunity for close views and photography.

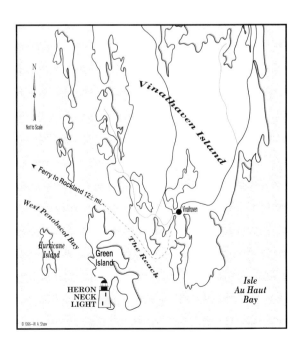

Indian Island Light:

Located at the eastern end of Rockport Harbor, this is no longer a functioning light. It was originally built in 1851, began operation in 1875 and has been privately owned since 1933. A distant view of this lighthouse is possible from the Rockport Marine Park or from the Beauchamp Point area but it is best photographed by boat.

Lobster buoys, Rockport Harbor

Directions: In Rockport at the intersection of U.S. 1 and ME 90, turn east onto West Street. Continue to Pascals Avenue and turn left, **crossing** the Goose River Bridge. Turn around and bear left just past the bridge into the Rockport Marine Park entrance (clearly marked). There is a parking area down the hill. **Or..** From Camden, follow Chestnut St. then Russell Ave. to Beauchamp Point. The road becomes a dirt road and, although narrow, there are areas to park. The area is lovely and the lighthouse can be seen in the distance.

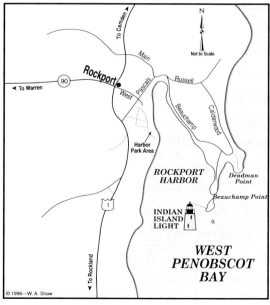

66

Two Bush Island Light:

Located just outside the west side of Penobscot Bay, almost directly south of Owl's Head Light, this light marks the north end of Two Bush Channel and the east side entrance to Muscle Ridge Channel, a principal sea lane to west Penobscot Bay. The light was built in 1897 and automated in 1963. Because no one could be found to take over maintenance of the station buildings, the Coast Guard in 1970 allowed the Green Berets to blow up the keeper's house as a demolition exercise. The light can only be photographed by air or boat.

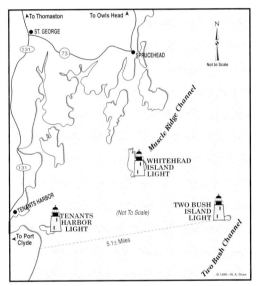

Matinicus Rock Light:

Matinicus Rock is an isolated, barren 30-acre rock about five miles southeast of Matinicus Island, 25 miles from Rockland, the nearest port. The lighthouse, located on the south side of the Rock, is probably the most isolated station along the Maine coast, halfway between Monhegan Island and Mt. Desert Island and 22 miles south of the entrance to Penobscot Bay. This location experiences some of the most violent Atlantic weather, is fogbound approximately 20% of the year and is continuously scoured by waves. The Rock is now a nesting area for a variety of seabirds including the previously endangered Atlantic puffin.

Twin wooden towers were built in 1827 which were replaced in 1848 with twin granite towers, both of which were rebuilt in 1857. The north light was discontinued in 1883, but the single light proved unsatisfactory and in 1888 the second light was reinstated. In 1924 Matinicus Rock became a single light station (north light again discontinued) by government order, as did other two-light stations. Following a violent storm in 1950, the station's outbuildings and old keeper's house were removed; the light was automated in 1983.

Although there are many tales of heroism by the keepers of Matinicus Rock Light, the best known is that of 17-year-old Abbie Burgess. She is credited with saving her three sisters and mother during a violent storm in January 1856. With her father gone to the mainland for provisions, Abbie took her family into the base of the lighthouse for safety as the storm swept away the keeper's house. While the storm kept her father away for a month, Abbie tended the lights and cared for her family. She later married the son of the light keeper who replaced her father and was appointed assistant keeper at Matinicus Rock.

Abbie, her husband and four children were transferred to the Whitehead Light station in 1875 where they served for 15 years. At the foot of her grave in Forest Hill Cemetery (off ME 73 between South Thomaston and St. George) is a small stone replica of a lighthouse.

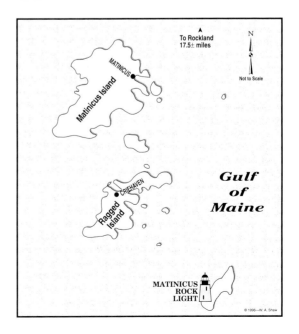

The lighthouse may be photographed
only by boat or by air.

69

Rockland Breakwater Light:

Located at the end of a 0.8 mile-long stone jetty extending from Jameson Point, this light was originally built in 1888. Construction of the breakwater began in 1881 and was completed in 1889. Piecemeal allocation of funds required that a makeshift light be moved and re-established at the unfinished end of the breakwater each time work was temporarily suspended. The present light was built in 1902 after completion of the breakwater; it was automated in 1964 and underwent major renovations in 1990.

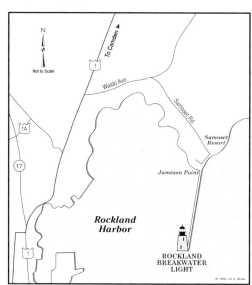

Directions: From U.S. Route 1, turn onto Waldo Avenue (Baptist Church, "Samoset Resort" sign). Continue for about 0.5 mile, turning right at Samoset road. The road ends at parking area. The breakwater, to the left of a small park area, leads about 0.8 mile out to the lighthouse. The Maine State Ferries from Rockland to Vinalhaven and North Haven pass close to this light. Additionally, Rockland is home to many of Maine's windjammers. A trip aboard any of these vessels takes you by Rockland Breakwater light and oftentimes other lighthouses in the Penobscot Bay and Mt. Desert Island area, according to time, tide, weather and whimsey of the captain.

70

Rockland Harbor Southwest:

This light was established as a local aid to navigation in 1987, marking Seal Ledge and shallow water south and southwest of the ledge. Built by a lighthouse enthusiast over a six-year period, the lighthouse is privately owned.

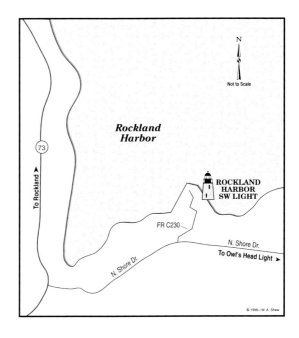

Directions: Take U.S. Route 1 to Thomaston, turning south onto ME 73. Continue about one mile past a "Welcome to Owl's Head" sign and turn left to North Shore Drive then continue east about 0.5 mile to FR C230 (a narrow dirt road marked with a small sign). The lighthouse is at the end of the lane adjacent to the owner's home.

Owl's Head Light:

On a promontory south of Rockland Harbor in Penobscot Bay, this short, stubby lighthouse is only 20 feet tall yet stands 100 feet above the water and was placed in service in September, 1825 to aid schooners transporting lime to Europe. Isaac Stearns was the first lightkeeper. Owl's Head light marks the heavily trafficked entry to Rockland Harbor and is on the National Register of Historic Places.

This light also has had its share of tales; in particular a keeper Augustus Hamer's dog Spot made his contribution to lighthouse history. In the 1930s Spot was credited with guiding the Matinicus mailboat safely past the peninsula. Although the dog had been taught how to ring the fogbell when boats passed near the rocks at Owl's head, the rope was buried in the snow. By barking constantly until he heard the boat whistle acknowledge it had cleared the rocks, the boat was headed safely to Rockland Harbor. Legend allows that Spot is buried near the present light and foghorn.

Directions: From U.S. Route 1 in Thomaston/Rockland, turn south onto ME 73 and continue about two miles, turning left onto North Shore Drive. Go about 2.5 miles, turning left just past the Owl's Head post office, onto Main Street. Continue to Lighthouse Road (marked) and turn left; the road becomes a dirt road and leads to a parking and picnic area. A short walk takes you to the lighthouse. The keeper's house is occupied by a Coast Guard family.

Ferries, harbor tour boats, windjammers and charter boat excursions all pass this light.

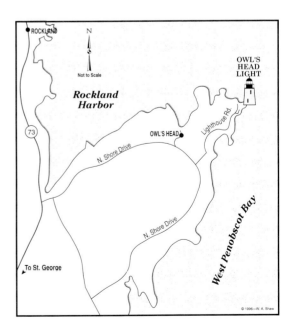

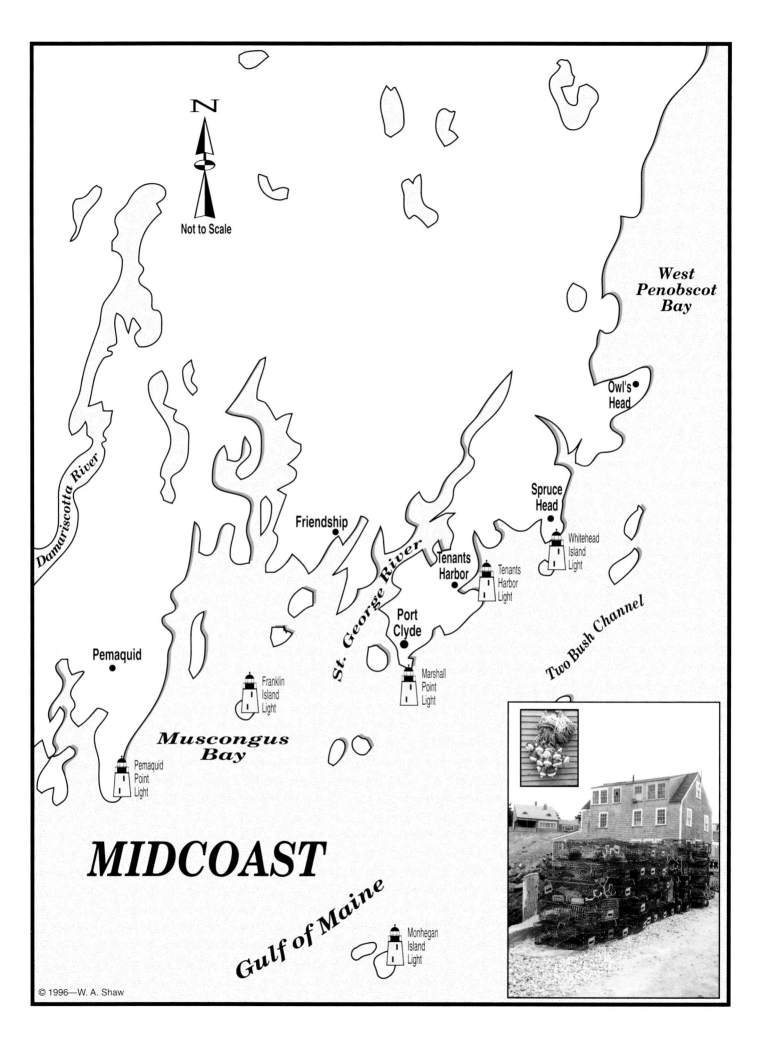

N
Not to Scale

West
Penobscot
Bay

Damariscotta River

Owl's
Head

Spruce
Head

Whitehead
Island
Light

Friendship

Tenants
Harbor

Tenants
Harbor
Light

St. George River

Port
Clyde

Pemaquid

Franklin
Island
Light

Marshall
Point
Light

Two Bush Channel

*Muscongus
Bay*

Pemaquid
Point
Light

MIDCOAST

Gulf of Maine

Monhegan
Island
Light

Whitehead Light:

President Thomas Jefferson ordered this lighthouse built in 1807; it was rebuilt in 1852. Located on a small island near Tenant's Harbor, this light marks the entrance to the Muscle Ridge Channel. Because this area is covered in fog approximately 20% of the year, a fog signal was installed in 1839. The signal was continuously operated by a striking mechanism which was wound, then driven by the rise and fall of the tide. Whitehead was the first Maine light station to have a one-room school house and teacher, with children from nearby islands in attendance. The light was automated in 1982.

Tales associated with this light include that of two shipwrecked sailors who froze to death on the island in 1805; their graves remain on the island. Another involves the initial keeper who tried to supplement his income by selling surplus whale oil obtained by falsifying his usage records. Finally, this is the lightstation to which heroine Abbie Burgess and her family were relocated in 1875 from Matinicus Rock. (Note lighthouse location on Tenants Harbor map, following page).

Tenants Harbor Light:

Now known as "Jamie Wyeth's place", the light is located at the east end of Southern Island at the harbor's entrance. The light was built in 1857 and discontinued in 1933 when it was sold to Andrew Wyeth. His son, Jamie, now owns the property. The lighthouse and keeper's dwelling have been restored and beautifully maintained; the pyramidal bell tower serves as a studio.

This lighthouse and Whitehead Island lighthouse can only be seen by boat or by air.

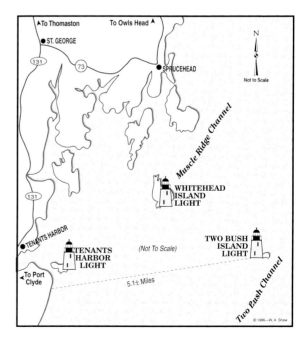

Marshall Point Light:

Marking the eastern side of the south entrance to Port Clyde Harbor, this light was built in 1832 and rebuilt in 1857. The brick and granite lighthouse is connected to the shore by a wooden walkway and resembles the Isle au Haut and Ram Island Lights. In 1980 the light was automated and the keeper's house and grounds acquired by the Town of St. George.

The Marshall Point Restoration Committee was formed in 1986 and in 1988 the keeper's house was placed on the National Register of Historic Places. Grants of more than $100,000 from the National Park Service Bicentennial Lighthouse Fund, matched by the Town of St. George and public contributions, were used by the St. George Historical Society to restore the keeper's residence. The Marshall Point Lighthouse Museum displays memorabilia relating to the town and three area lighthouses: Tenant's Harbor, Whitehead and Marshall Point. Most recently the summer kitchen has been rebuilt as an addition to the museum; future plans include rebuilding of the bell tower and outbuildings.

(Continued, following page)

Marshall Point Light: (continued)

Inside the keeper's house/museum; the case displays miniature lobster buoys identifying local fishermen.

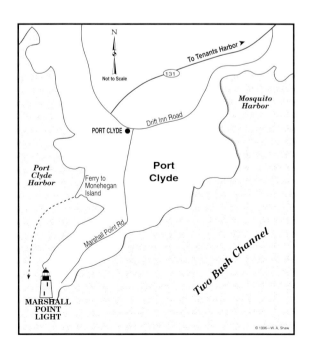

Directions: From U.S. Route 1 in Thomaston, take ME 131 south through St. George and Tenant's Harbor to Port Clyde. Turn left at the "Marshall Point Museum" sign (Dick Cliff Road). Continue up the hill, passing another sign for the museum, and turn right onto Marshall Point Road. Pass a "Dead End" sign and two stone pillars on either side of the narrowing road. The road ends at the lighthouse parking area. The passenger ferry Elizabeth Ann out of Port Clyde to Monhegan Island passes this light.

Franklin Island Light:

Five miles offshore from the village of Friendship, Maine, this light was built in 1855 to replace a day marker placed as a navigational aid in 1807. The lighthouse is located on the northwest side of Franklin Island in Muscongus Bay. Only the light tower remains; the keeper's house and outbuildings were dismantled by the Coast Guard when the light was automated in 1967.

This light can be photographed only by boat or air. Steve Lash of Friendship graciously gave me a ride to the light in his lobster boat.

81

Pemaquid Point Light:

Offering at once some of the most majestic, stark and striking scenery on the Maine coast, this lighthouse sits atop unique rock formations which reflect the result of waves pounding this area in strong storms. Commissioned in 1827 by John Quincy Adams, this light is located at the west side of the entrance to Muscongus Bay. The original lighthouse was of faulty construction and therefore rebuilt in 1857. During the years 1903-1917 four major shipwrecks occurred on the rocks at Pemaquid Point. The light, visible on a clear day for 14 miles, was automated in 1934 and the fogbell removed at that time. The keeper's house now houses the Fishermen's Museum which is operated by the Town of Bristol, displaying artifacts of Maine lighthouses and the fishing/lobster industry.

"Near this site on August 14, 1635 John Cogswell and family from Westbury Leigh, Wietshire, England first set foot in America. They arrived on the ship *Angel Gabriel,* which was wrecked here on the following day in a violent storm. The family settled in Ipswich, Massachusetts."

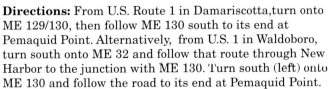

Directions: From U.S. Route 1 in Damariscotta, turn onto ME 129/130, then follow ME 130 south to its end at Pemaquid Point. Alternatively, from U.S. 1 in Waldoboro, turn south onto ME 32 and follow that route through New Harbor to the junction with ME 130. Turn south (left) onto ME 130 and follow the road to its end at Pemaquid Point.

To view the lighthouse by boat, cruises are available out of Boothbay Harbor or from Maine Maritime Museum in Bath.

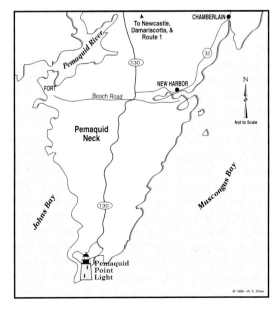

Monhegan Island Light:

Ten miles off the coast, Monhegan Island was originally settled in 1614, offering a safe haven from Indians. The island is 1.5 miles long, 0.5 miles wide and represents Maine's first fishing village, with its permanent residents still primarily engaged in fishing and lobstering. To avoid over fishing, Monhegan lobster season is limited to the winter months, January to June, with New Year's Day (or thereabouts depending on the weather) being "Trap Day", one of the year's major occasions. For their work in the most challenging weather conditions, Monhegan fishermen benefit from significantly higher lobster prices during this time.

The lighthouse, located near the center of the island at the island's highest elevation, was first lit in 1824 and rebuilt in 1850. Since Monhegan Island was the first point sighted on most trans-Atlantic voyages and a well-known landmark for seafarers, it was logical a lighthouse should be located here. This lighthouse is the second highest above water on the Maine coast at 178 feet; only Seguin is higher at 180 feet. In 1959 the light was automated and is now controlled from the Coast Guard station on Manana Island, across the harbor. The keeper's house is now a museum.

Reportedly more than six hundred varieties of wild flowers can be found on Monhegan, with more than two hundred bird species logged. The island also has become a summer art colony, and has, in past years, attracted writers, naturalists and artists including Andrew and Jamie Wyeth, Rockwell Kent, George Bellows and Andrew Winter.

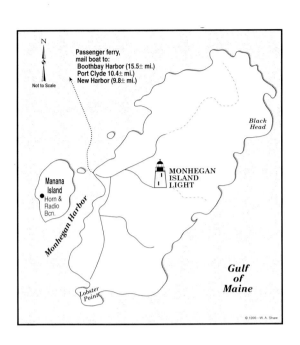

Directions: Monhegan Island is reached by air or by boat from either Boothbay Harbor, New Harbor or Port Clyde:

Monhegan Island

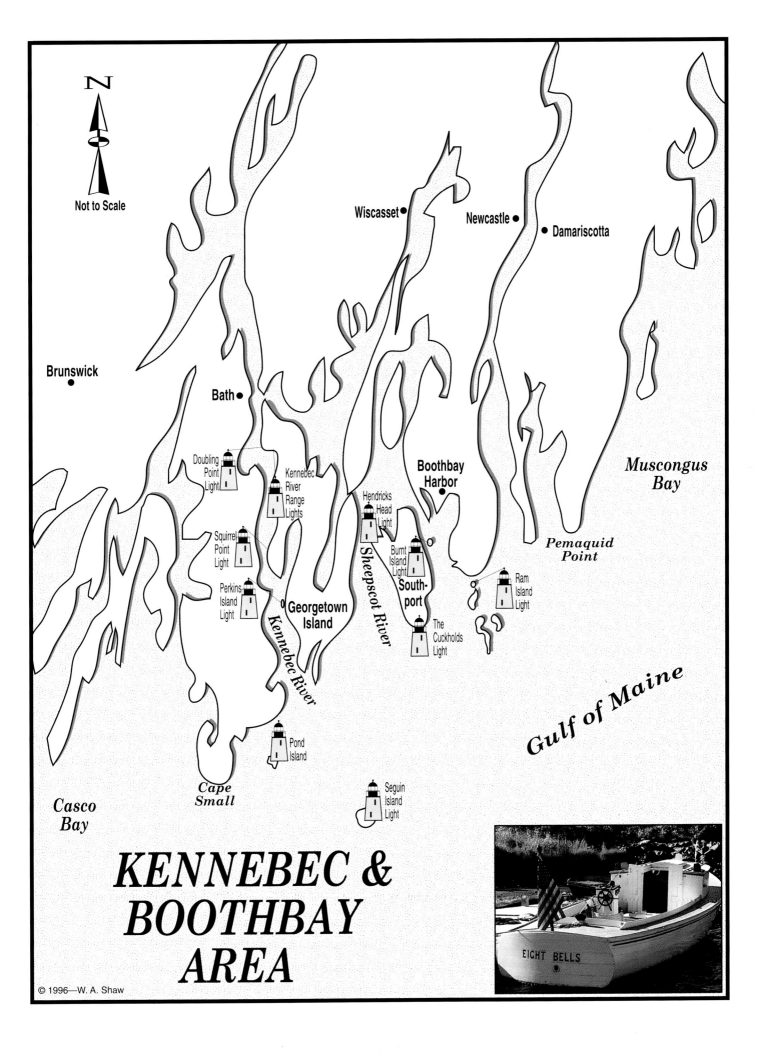

N

Not to Scale

Wiscasset •

Newcastle •   • Damariscotta

Brunswick
•

Bath •

*Muscongus
Bay*

Doubling
Point
Light

Kennebec
River
Range
Lights

**Boothbay
Harbor** •

Hendricks
Head
Light

Squirrel
Point
Light

*Pemaquid
Point*

Burnt
Island
Light

Ram
Island
Light

Perkins
Island
Light

**Georgetown
Island**

Sheepscot River

**South-
port**

Kennebec River

The
Cuckholds
Light

Gulf of Maine

Pond
Island

*Cape
Small*

Seguin
Island
Light

*Casco
Bay*

KENNEBEC &
BOOTHBAY
AREA

EIGHT BELLS

The Cuckholds Light:

In 1892 a stone fog signal house was built on this small island less than a mile off the tip of Southport Island and the village of Newagen. A light tower was added atop the original signal house in 1907. The light was automated in 1975 and the property abandoned; the keeper's house and other outbuildings were subsequently swept away in a winter storm. The light can be seen from ME 27 in Newagen but is best photographed from a tour boat out of Boothbay Harbor.

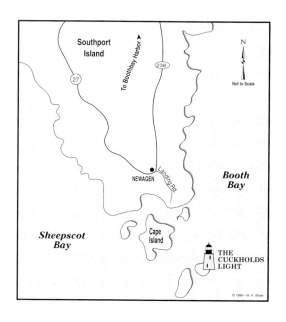

Directions: From U.S. Route 1, take ME 27 south into Boothbay Harbor. Continue on RT 27 to Southport Island to the Village of Newagen. At the post office ME 27 turns 90 degrees north into ME 238; bear southeast into a paved road with a "Town Landing" sign at the corner. Continue to a small parking area at the public pier. The lighthouse can be seen in the distance. Tour boats offer better photographic opportunities.

Burnt Island Light:

Located on the west side of the entrance to Boothbay Harbor, this lighthouse was built in 1821 and altered in 1888. The modifications were required because its light interfered with that from the Cuckholds light. After the changes were made ships were not attracted over the rocks at the Cuckholds which were in the path to Burnt Island Light. Ships were first guided by the Cuckholds light past the ledges there, then Burnt Island Light provided guidance for passage into Boothbay Harbor.

The light is best photographed from one of the tour boats from Boothbay Harbor although distant views are possible from the mainland on the east side of the harbor.

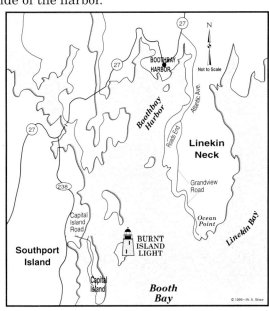

Directions: From U.S. Route 1, take ME 27 south into Boothbay Harbor. All tour boats will pass this light, some closer than others.

To view the light from shore: Take ME 27 (Townsend) north to Union St. Turn right then right again at Atlantic Ave. Continue past Lobster Cove Rd. and Roads End Rd. to Grand View Rd. The lighthouse may be seen from several points along that road heading to the Spruce Point Inn. **Or..** Take Commercial St. (one way) to the Tugboat Inn; the light can be seen from the docks there.

Ram Island Light:

Built in 1883, this light is located on Ram Island off Ocean Point on the eastern side of Boothbay Harbor. After automation in 1965, the station fell into disrepair; the long walkway originally bridging the lighthouse tower to the island rotted away. In 1977, the Coast Guard rebuilt the lighthouse and removed the remains of the tower-to-shore walkway.

The Grand Banks Schooner Museum Trust took over the keeper's house and outbuildings in 1985, undertaking repair and restoration of the buildings, including restoration of the interior of the house. The grounds are now well maintained by part time caretakers. The Grand Banks Schooner Museum is the restored *Sherman Zwicker* often on sojourn at the Maine Maritime Museum in Bath, Maine.

Arrangements to visit the light and island may be made through the Boothbay Railway Village. The Maine Maritime Museum also offers trips to the island (including landing); several tour boats out of Boothbay Harbor also pass this station. Alternatively, the light can be viewed in the distance from Ocean Point near Boothbay Harbor.

Directions: From U.S. 1 take ME 27 south to Boothbay Harbor. Then take ME 96 east and south to Ocean Point and follow the shoreline loop road. Along that road there are numerous points to view the lighthouse across Fisherman Island passage.

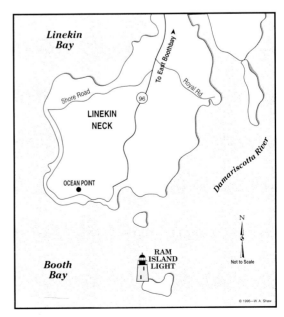

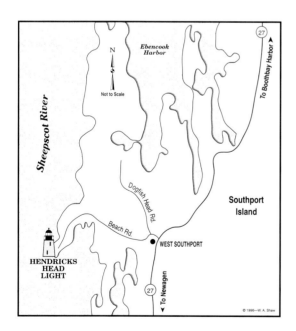

Directions: From U.S. Route 1, take ME 27 south into Boothbay Harbor. Continue on ME 27 to Southport Island. Bear right around a triangular intersection (Southport General Store on the right), then, as the road dips down, bear left at the "Beach Road" sign. Continue about 0.5 mile to the beach and parking area.

Hendricks Head Light:

The original light on the point of Southport Island on the east side of the mouth of the Sheepscot River was built in 1829. A fire required rebuilding of the keeper's house in 1875. The station was discontinued in 1933, sold to private owners, then re-established and automated in 1951. In 1991 the five-acre property was again sold to private owners who have carefully and accurately restored the structures to original appearance.

Two tales are associated with this station, one of an unusual rescue, another of an unidentified ghost.

Following a storm and shipwreck, a bundle washed ashore and was retrieved by the lightkeeper. The small package turned out to be an infant wrapped in a box between two feather mattresses for protection. The baby girl survived the ordeal and was adopted by the keeper and his wife when no other survivors were found.

Additionally, a keeper whose tenure included the years between the first and second world wars, reported the presence of an unknown woman walking in the area of the Southport post office. The postmaster also mentioned seeing the woman but neither had spoken to her. Her body was found the next day, weighted down with a flatiron. She was buried in Southport, her identity never known. Her ghostly figure has been reportedly seen walking the deserted beach in winter months, haunting the site where she committed suicide.

The light can be photographed from the beach in Southport or from a tour boat from Boothbay Harbor.

Seguin Island Light:

Maine's second lighthouse was built in 1795 to mark the mouth of the heavily travelled Kennebec River by order of President George Washington at a cost of $6300. The light has since been rebuilt twice, in 1820 and 1857; at 186 feet this light is the highest above water on the Maine coast and can be seen from a distance of 40 miles in clear weather. The present 53-foot granite light tower was necessary to accommodate the installation of Maine's only first-order Fresnel lens. Because of heavy fog often in this area, Seguin has one of the most powerful foghorns made. The light was automated in 1985.

Although the Coast Guard maintains the light, the island and keeper's quarters are managed by the Friends of Seguin Island, a nonprofit organization. By 1990 public contributions, grants from the Maine Historic Preservation Commission, National Park Service and matching fund programs had made possible restoration of the keeper's quarters to accommodate summertime caretakers. In August of 1993 the Friends of Seguin opened a small museum in the lower two rooms on the north side of the keeper's house. Restoration, repair and maintenance of the grounds and buildings are ongoing efforts by this group.

Located two miles south of the mouth of the Kennebec River, this light can be seen in the distance from the Popham Beach area. However, Maine Maritime Museum and the Friends group sponsor trips to the island during the summer. These trips include 1.5 hours on the island to explore the lighthouse, museum and grounds. There is no dock or pier landing; passengers are off-loaded into a skiff and taken to the beach. The climb to the lighthouse is fairly steep up a narrow path.

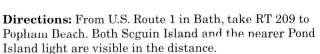

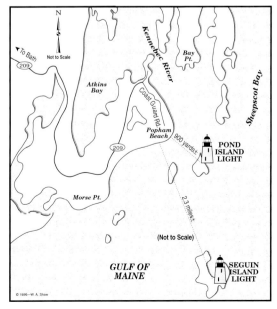

Directions: From U.S. Route 1 in Bath, take RT 209 to Popham Beach. Both Seguin Island and the nearer Pond Island light are visible in the distance.

* Maine Maritime Museum: From U.S. Route 1 in Bath, take the"Historic Bath"/Front St. exit, turning onto Washington St. Follow the signs past Bath Iron Works to the Museum (clearly marked): 243 Washington St., Bath, ME. 04530 (207) 443-6100 or (207) 443-1316.

95

Pond Island Light:

This light marks the east side entrance to the Kennebec River and is about two miles northwest of Seguin Island. The original stone tower was built in 1821, then rebuilt in 1855; it was automated in 1963 and all buildings removed.

The U.S. Fish and Wildlife Service now manages the 10-acre island as a migratory bird refuge. No excursions to land on the island are available although some of the Boothbay tour boats and the boats to Seguin Island from Maine Maritime Museum pass by this light. Rough seas in this area often make photographing this light difficult. The light can be seen in the distance from Popham Beach.

Directions: From U.S.Route 1 in Bath, ME., take ME 209 to Popham Beach. *Maine Maritime Museum-From U.S. Route 1 in Bath, take the "Historic Bath" exit. Turn onto Washington St and follow the signs past Bath Iron Works to the Museum (clearly marked), 243 Washington St.

*Custom boat charter arrangements in the Harpswell/Bath/ Phippsburg/Georgetown area will provide the only opportunity for a close view of the light.

Perkins Island Light:

Built in 1898 on the eastern side of the Kennebec River, this light is now on the "endangered list" as the property and light are not maintained. The station and property were transferred to the Town of Georgetown in 1973 but little has been done to improve the buildings. The light may be seen across the river from the village of Parker Head; best photographs are taken by boat.

Directions: From US Route 1, take High Street/RT 209 to Phippsburg. Turn left just past the post office and library into Parker Head Road. This road follows the river into Parker Head; turn left downhill into a public landing road. Perkins Island light is directly across the Kennebec River in Georgetown. An excursion boat from Maine Maritime Museum or tour boat from Boothbay Harbor which passes all of the Kennebec River lighthouses offers the best views.

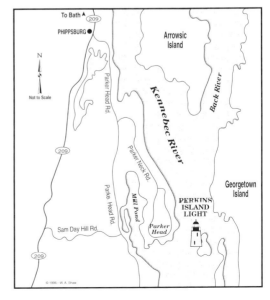

Squirrel Point Light:

Located on the southwest point of Arrowsic Island, this light was built in 1898 and is similar in appearance to Perkins Island Light and Doubling Point Light (both on the Kennebec River). The light was automated in 1982. The keeper's house is now privately owned and is being restored.

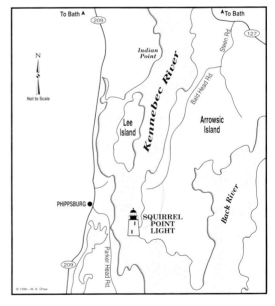

Directions: The light may be seen directly across the river from Phippsburg on ME 209. Alternatively, from U. S. Route 1 just north of Bath, take RT 127 toward Arrowsic. Continue for about 4.5 miles; just before reaching the Georgetown-Arrowsic bridge, turn right onto Steen Road, then bear left onto Bald Head Road (dirt). This road ends after about 0.5 mile in a small parking area. From that area is a footpath to the lighthouse (about 3/4 mile). The path begins straight ahead from the parking area; listen for the sound of water and look for the shoreline. After crossing a small, wooden bridge the path through the woods to the lighthouse is marked with faint yellow blazes. Keep the water (Kennebec River) to your right on the way to the lighthouse and on your left when returning.

Kennebec River Range Lights:

This light, built in 1908 and formerly called Doubling Point Range Light, consists of two wooden towers with the rear tower 235 feet behind the one on shore. These are the only range lights in Maine. Straight alignment of the lights indicates to vessels the middle of the river channel on approach to Fiddler Reach, a sharp double bend in the river just beyond at Doubling Point.

Beginning in 1938, efforts were made to consolidate and automate the series of Kennebec River lighthouses. First, the Doubling Point keeper's house and grounds were sold to a private owner and the keeper of the Doubling Point Range Lights took over responsibility for that light. In 1979 these lights were automated and the keeper of at Squirrel Point Light given responsibility for all the Kennebec lights.

Finally in 1981 the Coast Guard moved the keeper from Squirrel Point back to Doubling Point Range Light Station. In 1982 the station was renamed Kennebec River Light Station and was the first to be tended by a woman resident keeper, followed by her husband until 1990. All Kennebec River lighthouses, from Doubling Point to Perkins Island, are now automated.

Rear Light

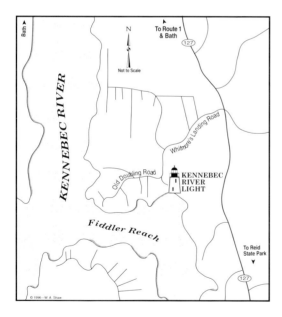

Front Light

Directions: From U.S. Route 1 in Woolwich, turn south onto ME 127. After about 1.5 miles, just before the Arrowsic Town Hall, turn right onto Whitmore Landing Rd to Doubling Point Road (marked). At the first fork, turn left into Doubling Point Rd; bear left at the next fork and continue on the narrow lane to the lights. There is a boardwalk leading to the lighthouses. Alternatively these lights are seen on Kennebec River trips from Boothbay Harbor or Maine Maritime Museum.

Doubling Point Light:

Ships from the Atlantic are guided into the shipbuilding town of Bath, Maine by this light. One of four on the Kennebec River, the lighthouse was built in 1898 and is closest to Bath near the upper end of Fiddler Reach. The light is privately owned and may be photographed by boat or seen from a distance across the river on RT 209 to Phippsburg.

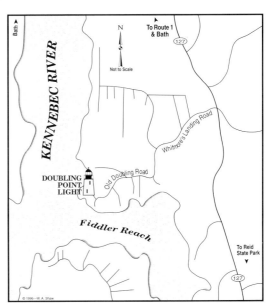

Directions: From U.S. Route 1 in Bath, take the High Street/ RT 209 exit to Phippsburg. The light may be seen across the river just a short distance south of Bath. Alternatively, from U.S. 1 in Woolwich, turn south onto RT 127 and continue to Georgetown. Continue on ME 127 past the junction with the road to Reid State Park and into the village of Five Islands, then straight ahead to the lobster coop wharf. The light can be seen across the Sheepscot River about one mile away. Excursion boats offer close views of this light.

101

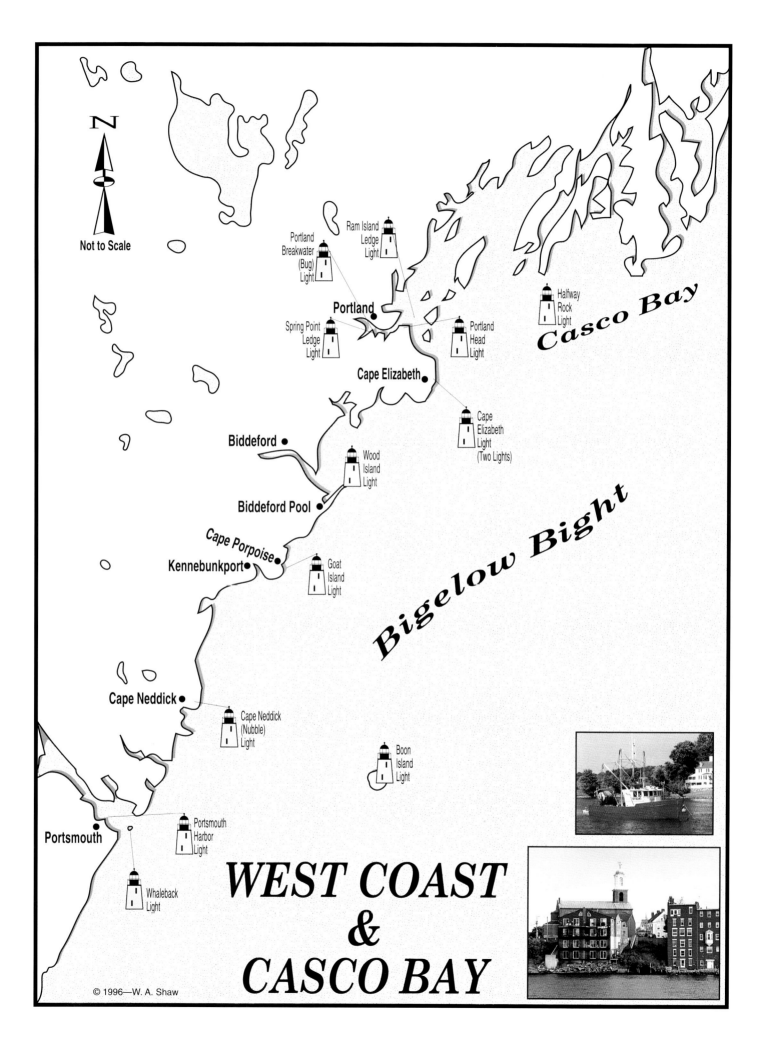

N

Not to Scale

Portland Breakwater (Bug) Light

Ram Island Ledge Light

Halfway Rock Light

Casco Bay

Portland

Spring Point Ledge Light

Portland Head Light

Cape Elizabeth

Cape Elizabeth Light (Two Lights)

Biddeford

Wood Island Light

Biddeford Pool

Bigelow Bight

Cape Porpoise

Kennebunkport

Goat Island Light

Cape Neddick

Cape Neddick (Nubble) Light

Boon Island Light

Portsmouth Harbor Light

Portsmouth

Whaleback Light

WEST COAST
&
CASCO BAY

Halfway Rock Light:

Named because it is halfway between Cape Elizabeth
and Cape Small, this barren three-acre ledge is
located about 11 miles northeast of Portland in a busy
shipping lane. Construction of the light was begun in
1870 but bad weather and funding glitches prevented
completion until 1871. The station suffered substantial damage in storms of 1962 and again in 1972. The
latter storm washed away the outbuildings and
equipment and required helicopter evacuation of the
crew. Only the light tower, entryway and helicopter
pad remain. The light must be photographed from the
air or by boat.

Directions: Although on a clear day this light may be
seen in the distance from aboard a Casco Bay Cruise
boat, these excursions do not allow for close views or
photography. A custom boat charter may be arranged
out of Harpswell. A distant view is possible by taking
RT 24 south from Brunswick at the Cook's Corner
intersection to Orr's & Bailey Islands. Continue to a
small parking area and gift shop at the end of the
road.

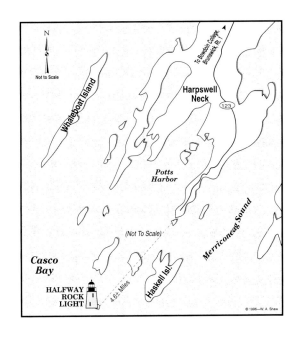

Ram Island Ledge Light:

This light sits on jagged rocks at the north side of the entrance to Portland Harbor. At high tide the ledges are entirely covered and were the cause of many shipwrecks until a lighthouse was built here in 1905. Gray granite blocks used to construct the tower were cut from quarries on Vinalhaven, Maine and give the lighthouse the appearance of being much older than it is. The light was converted from kerosene to electricity in 1958 and automated in1959.This light can be

seen offshore from Fort Williams Park in Cape Elizabeth. Some of the Casco Bay boat trips will afford a distant view or a charter trip can be arranged for close photography.

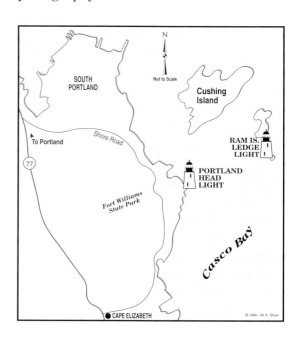

Directions: From U.S. Route 1 in Portland, take the ME 77 exit (Congress St) and follow that route through Portland, past the harbor to South Portland, then into Cape Elizabeth. Turn left at the "Portland Head Light" sign onto Shore Road; continue to Fort Williams State Park and Portland Head Light.The Casco Bay cruises and harbor trips offer distant views of this light; a custom boat charter is the only way to get close photographs.

Portland Breakwater (Bug) Light:

First built in 1855 at the end of a breakwater about 0.5 mile into the harbor, this light was rebuilt in 1875 and a keeper's house added next to the tower in 1889. The unusual lighthouse design, petite with Corinthian columns, was created to resemble a 4th century (B.C.) Greek monument. The light was automated in 1934.

To accommodate World War II shipbuilding, land was filled in from shore to the light station eliminating the breakwater and making the light obsolete. The light was extinguished in 1942. In 1989, after long standing unattended, significant repair and restoration were accomplished with money from the National Park Service Bicentennial Lighthouse Fund, Maine Historic Preservation Commission and South Portland/Cape Elizabeth community organizations. This unique light is listed on the National Register of Historic Places.

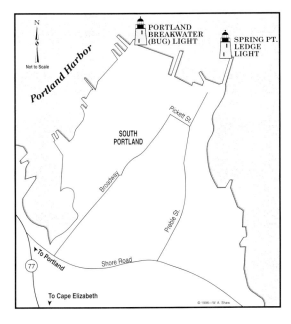

Directions: Take RT 77 from South Portland to Broadway. Turn east on Broadway and continue to Pickett Street. Turn left onto Pickett Street and follow that road around the warehouses then bear left to the parking area for the South Portland Public Landing. Entrance to the parking area is free unless launching a boat. Walk along the fence toward the landing; to the right is a walkway to the light. Tour boats from Portland also offer good views.

Spring Point Ledge Light:

When this light was originally built in 1855 it was offshore from Fort Preble, marking the west side of the main channel to Portland Harbor. After being rebuilt in 1855 and again in 1875, the tower was completely replaced in 1897 and is similar in appearance to the Goose Rocks and Lubec Channel lights. An automated electric lamp replaced the kerosene-fueled light in 1934. In 1951 the 900-foot breakwater was constructed from shore to the light tower.

This lighthouse is easily accessible by car and it is possible to walk out on the breakwater to the lighthouse. Tour boats from Portland also offer good views of the light.

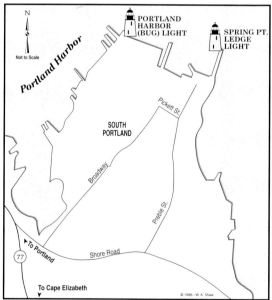

Directions: From ME 77 in Portland, turn east onto Broadway and continue to Pickett Street. Turn right onto Pickett and follow it to the end. Turn left onto Fort Road which ends at Fort Preble (now Southern Maine Vocational Training Institute) and a parking area. The light and breakwater are immediately ahead just to the right.

Portland Head Light:

The patriarch of Maine's lighthouses marks the state's busiest harbor. Built on order of George Washington in 1791, Portland Head Light is Maine's oldest light and boasts a combination of historic significance, beauty and location making it possibly the most visited, photographed and painted lighthouse in the United States.

At the time construction of this light was begun in 1787, Maine was still a part of the Massachusetts Bay Colony. John Hancock was then governor of the Colony and authorized the work. The Federal government took over management of lighthouses in 1789 and completed the construction of the 80-foot tower in 1791. President George Washington then appointed the first keeper, Captain Joseph Greenleaf.

This lighthouse has witnessed many shipwrecks and has a substantial list of notable names associated with it. *The Bohemian* was split apart on the rocks nearby in 1864 and among the survivors was John E. Fitzgerald, maternal grandfather of President John F. Kennedy, Robert and Edward Kennedy. Fitzgerald later became mayor of Boston, known as "Honey Fitz". In 1886, the ship *Annie C. Maguire* was shipwrecked on Christmas Eve; there is a marker painted on the rocks in her memory. Additionally, Henry Wadsworth Longfellow found the tranquil beauty of the setting well suited to writing poetry.

The light was automated in August, 1989, a major event in concert with National Lighthouse Day. Renovation of the keeper's quarters was accomplished in 1990 to create a museum, dedicated in 1992, now operated by the Town of Cape Elizabeth. Portland Head Light is adjacent to Fort Williams State Park.

(Continued, following pages)

Portland Head Light

Portland Head Light

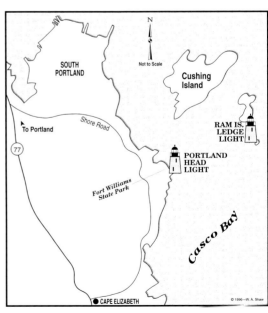

Directions: From I-95, 295, or U.S. 1, take ME 77 to Cape Elizabeth (clearly marked). Turn east onto Shore Road and follow that road to Fort Williams State Park (several "Portland Head Light" signs direct you). The light can also be photographed from a tour boat out of Portland .

109

Cape Elizabeth Light (Two Lights):

The Cape Elizabeth lights were built in 1828, the second location in Maine to have two light towers (Matinicus Rock also at one time had twin lights). The west light was discontinued in 1855 by the Lighthouse Board. Subsequently, local fishermen and lobstermen protested the inactivation of the light, whereupon it was reestablished in 1855. To aid in daytime recognition, four horizontal red bands were painted on the east tower and a single, broad vertical red stripe added to the west tower. Both towers were rebuilt in 1874.

The government in 1924 ordered that all coastal light stations be reduced to single lights and the west tower was dismantled. It has subsequently been sold to several private owners, renovated and restored.

Visible for 27 nautical miles, the active, functioning east tower is the most powerful on the New England coast at four million candle power. The keeper's house and grounds are privately owned. This lighthouse was the subject of a painting by Edward Hopper; that painting was pictured on a 1970 postage stamp commemorating Maine's 150th anniversary.

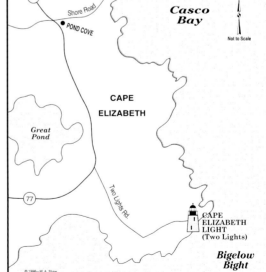

Directions: From Portland/South Portland, take RT 77 to Cape Elizabeth. Continue about four miles, then bear left onto Two Lights Road (Two Lights State Park is to the right). Continue for about 1.5 miles, turning left at Two Lights Terrace; the light and keeper's house (private property) are on a knoll at the end of the road immediately to the right. The lighthouse also may be photographed from a park area at the end of Two Lights Road.

Wood Island Light:

Legend says that this island is haunted by the ghost of a murder victim. The tale involves a half-hearted lobsterman who shot and killed a local law officer, then turned himself in to the light keeper. Frightened by the drunken man waving a rifle at him, the keeper told him to turn himself in to police. Instead, the lobsterman returned to his squatter's shack and committed suicide. The ghost of the murdered law officer is said to haunt the island still.

Just off the village of Biddeford Pool, this light marks the entrance to the Saco River. The light, built in 1808 and rebuilt in 1858 on the east end of Wood Island, was automated in 1986. Recently the Coast Guard has completed repair and partial restoration of the tower and keeper's house. Since 1976 most of the 36-acre island has been managed by the Maine Audubon Society; eight acres and buildings belong to the station. The light can be seen in the distance from shore but is best photographed by boat.

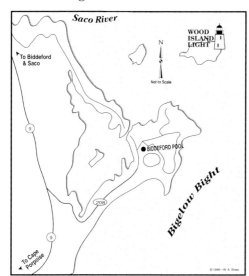
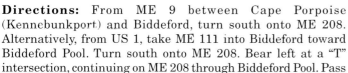

Directions: From ME 9 between Cape Porpoise (Kennebunkport) and Biddeford, turn south onto ME 208. Alternatively, from US 1, take ME 111 into Biddeford toward Biddeford Pool. Turn south onto ME 208. Bear left at a "T" intersection, continuing on ME 208 through Biddeford Pool. Pass the firestation and continue about 0.5 mile— the road makes a right angle to follow the shoreline. Just before that turn there is a gate and a path along side it to a well-marked footpath. The walk to the shoreline is along the Audubon Trail next to the golf course with the lighthouse visible shortly ahead across the inlet.

Goat Island Light:

Notable for being Maine's last manned light station, this lighthouse was not automated until 1990. The light, built in 1833 and rebuilt in 1859, is located at the southwest end of Goat Island near the entrance to Cape Porpoise Harbor. Because this station was used as a security post when former President George Bush was in residence at Walker's Point in Kennebunkport, the structures are well maintained.

In 1992 the Coast Guard leased the light station to the Kennebunkport Conservation Trust, a community service organization. The intent is to solicit contributions for upkeep of the buildings which will be used for educational programs. The lighthouse can be seen in the distance from the wharf at Cape Porpoise or tour boats out of Kennebunkport pass this light.

Directions: From I-95 take the Kennebunkport exit, follow ME 35 into Kennebunk. Take ME 9A south to Kennebunkport (or from US 1. take RT 9A also). Route 9A becomes RT 9; continue through Kennebunkport to Cape Porpoise Center. Where ME 9 makes a 90-degree turn left, instead **bear right** onto Pier Road which ends at the wharf. The light is offshore to the southeast. Better photographs are possible from a tour boat out of Kennebunkport.

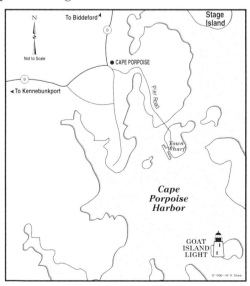

113

Cape Neddick (Nubble) Light:

Among the most appealing and photographed lighthouses on the Maine coast, this light was first illuminated in July, 1879. The light was automated in 1987; the island and station are leased to the Town of York and a trust has been established to ensure ongoing maintenance of the property.

Unique to this light tower are the miniature cast iron lighthouses atop the posts on the railing surrounding the lantern room. Also distinguishing the Nubble light was a past feline resident who, at 19 pounds, reportedly attracted as many interested tourists as did the lighthouse itself. The cat was allegedly the best mouser in Maine, regularly swimming the channel to visit briefly with mainland friends then returning to the lighthouse to deal with the mice.

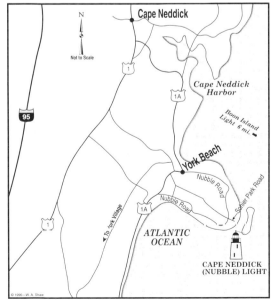

Directions: From I-95 or U.S. Route 1 in York, take U.S. 1A to York Beach, continuing to Nubble Road (marked with a small "Nubble Light" sign). Follow this road to Sohier Park and the parking area.

Summer

Fall

Winter

Spring

**Change of season at
Cape Neddick (Nubble) Light**

Boon Island Light:

Standing on a small, rocky and barren island about 6.5 miles southeast of Cape Neddick, this light is clearly one of the most isolated. Severe storms, typical of this area, have swept away numerous light towers on this ledge. The first light was established in 1800 but the flimsy wooden structure was destroyed by a storm in 1804 then replaced with a stone tower that year. That tower was replaced in 1812 only to be destroyed by a storm in 1831.

Finally, the Lighthouse Board allowed that a much more sound, substantial structure was required and, in 1855, built the present light tower. At 133 feet, this lighthouse is the tallest on the Maine Coast; it is 25 wide at the base, 12 feet wide at the top. The name, "Boon", refers to packages of food and clothing left on the island by mainland fisherman for use by any shipwreck victim able to get onto the rocks.

This island is continually pounded by the sea and a storm in 1978 occasioned the final removal of personnel from the station. During that storm granite boulders were tossed about and the keepers house and outbuildings destroyed as five feet of water inundated the island. The two keepers were rescued by helicopter the following day and the light subsequently automated. Although best photographed by boat, the light can be seen in clear weather from Cape Neddick.

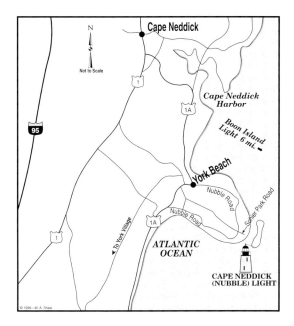

Directions: From I-95 or U.S. Route 1 in York, take U.S. 1A to York Beach, continuing to Nubble Road (marked with a small "Nubble Light" sign). Follow this road to Sohier Park and the parking area.

Whaleback Light:

Located at the northeast side of Portsmouth Harbor at the entrance to the Piscataqua River, this light is in Maine waters although guarding the entrance to the New Hampshire harbor. The original lighthouse was built in 1831 and replaced in 1831. That light lasted almost 40 years despite the combination of faulty initial construction and repeated severe storms. In 1868 storm damage was irreparable and the present lighthouse completed in 1872; the base of the original tower still stands. Whaleback was automated in 1964. Although the light can be seen from Ft. Constitution in Newcastle, NH. and from Ft. Foster in Kittery, Maine, it is best photographed by boat.

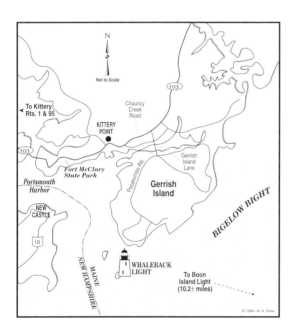

Directions: From I-95 or U.S. Route 1 in Kittery, take ME 103 east. Continue on ME 103 past the entrance to the Portsmouth Naval Shipyard and the entrance to Ft. McClary. Pass the intersection with Hoyts Island Road, bear right to Chauncy Creek Road, then right again at Gerrish Island Lane. Cross over the bridge and bear right at Pocahontas Road to the park entrance. **Alternatively:**

From I-95 or U.S. Route 1, take the waterfront exit and/ or follow the signs to Strawberry Banke area. Follow Marcy Street (RT 1B) through this area toward Newcastle, the road becomes New Castle Avenue. Continue on 1B into New Castle to Wentworth Avenue. Turn left (Ft. Constitution Historic Site sign), then bear right to the parking area.

Portsmouth Harbor Light:

One of America's twelve colonial lighthouses, this light was built during the years 1782-84 at Fort Constitution. The area was originally named Fort William and Mary and was a British stronghold guarding the harbor. The first overt act of the Revolutionary War occurred in this area as the colonists overpowered the British fort. At the end of the war the fort was renamed Fort Constitution. George Washington, Daniel Webster and General Lafayette were notable visitors to this lighthouse.

The present tower of cast iron was built in 1877. Although the lighthouse is on an active Coast Guard Station it is possible to tour the grounds and photograph the light; tour boats from Portsmouth also pass the light.

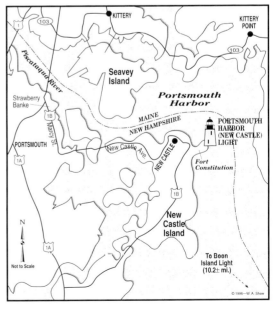

Directions: From I-95 or U.S. Route 1, take the waterfront exit and/or follow the signs to the Strawberry Banke area. Follow Marcy Street (RT 1B) through this area toward Newcastle; the road becomes New Castle Avenue. Continue on 1B into New Castle to Wentworth Avenue. Turn left (Ft. Constitution Historic Site sign), then bear right to the parking area. The light can also be seen in the distance from Ft. McClary in Kittery, Maine.

Scenic/Tour Boat and Charter Information:

Tour boats often pass lighthouses, sometimes offering excellent views. However, because lighthouses are only one element of these trips, close viewing/photography of the lighthouses is not usually accomplished. Rather, these excursions more likely will focus on sea birds, whales, or a general overview of the coastal area. A few "lighthouse trips" are available. Alternatively, custom charter arrangements can be made which enable you to choose a specific route, to get as close to the lighthouse(s) as possible and oftentimes, weather and seas permitting, to go ashore on the islands. Charter rates are typically on a per hour basis. The individuals listed for each area took me to the offshore lighthouses, sometimes more than once. All were extremely helpful, patient and accommodating in working with my schedule(s) and weather glitches requiring improvisation in routes and plans:

 ## Bold Coast and Downeast Coast Lights:

*__Andy Patterson, Bold Coast Charter Co.,__ P.O. Box 364, Cutler, ME. 04626 (207) 259-4484. Although trips on the __Barbara Frost__ to Machias Seal Island to view the puffins are his specialty, arrangements can be made for a trip to view the three lights in the area (Little River, Machias Seal Is., Libby Is.)

*__Barna & John Norton__ , RR 01- 990, Jonesport, ME. 04649 (207)-497-5933. Trips to Machias Seal Is. to view puffins—Libby Is.light seen on the way. Area lighthouse trips arranged on request.

__Air charter:__
* __Ace Aviation__: (In Belfast, Me. off U.S. Route 1.) P.O. Box 457, Belfast, Maine, 04915 (207)-338-2970.
* __Acadia Air,__ Hancock County/Bar Harbor Airport: Located in Trenton, Me. off ME 3. Only single engine planes available for "local" lighthouses, but they will arrange with Ace Aviation for flights to outermost lights. (207-667-5534).

Mt. Desert Area Lights:

*__Maine State Ferry Service__ (at Bass Harbor): (207) 244-3254
*__Frenchman Bay Boating Co.,__ 1 West St., Harbor Place, Bar Harbor, ME. 04609 (207) 288-3322
    * Capt.. Steven Pagels, P.O. Box 8, Cherryfield, ME. 04622. (207) 288-4585 (summer) or (207) 546-2927 (winter)

*__Whale-watching trips out of Bar Harbor__ usually head to feeding grounds in the Mt. Desert Rock area; Egg Rock Light and Bear Island Light are seen on the way out. However, because the route is determined by location of the whales, close views of Mt. Desert Rock light cannot always be guaranteed. __Acadian Whale Watcher__ (207) 288-9794, (207) 288-9776, or 1-800-421-3307

*In __Northeast Harbor:__
    Ferry and mail boat service to Cranberry Isles (__Sea Queen, Double B__) —Beal & Bunker, Inc. P.O. Box 33, Cranberry Isles, ME. 04625 (207) 244-3575. Passes Bear Island Light.

*In __Southwest Harbor:__
    Ferry to Cranberry Isles (June-September)—Cranberry Cove Boating Co. (__Island Queen__). (207) 244-5882. Passes Bear Island Light, trips to Baker Island.

**The two individuals listed below took me to all the lighthouses in the Mt. Desert/Bar Harbor area and beyond (including Pond, Nash, Petit Manan, Blue Hill Bay, Mt. Desert Rock Light and all in between) sometimes more than once. Both specialize is custom trips for photography and are able, weather and seas permitting, to take a skiff for landing at offshore lights.
    * __Wes Shaw, MDI Water Taxi__ (Northeast Harbor)—P.O. Box 18, Mt. Desert, ME. (207) 244-7312
    * __Fred Day, Ocean Image__—P.O. Box 162, Gt. Cranberry Isle, ME. 04625 (207) 244-9494. Northeast Harbor is the easiest embarkation point; others are Bar Harbor, Southwest Harbor, Bass Harbor. Alternatively, you can take the mailboat/ferry to Gt. Cranberry Isle where the __Polly Day__ is located, stay at the island B&B, and tour from there.

Mt. Desert Area (con't)

Air Charters:
*__Acadia Air,__ Hancock Co./ Bar Harbor Airport, (Just off RT 3 in Trenton) RD #1 Box 170F, Ellsworth, ME. 04605 (207)-667-5534.
*__Ace Aviation__, P.O. Box 457, Belfast, ME. (207)338-2970. (Just off U.S. Route 1 in Belfast--clearly marked)

 Eggemoggin Reach Lights:

* **Dave Zinn, Jericho Bay Charters** (*Lady Michelle*), P.O. Box 62, Deer Isle, ME. 04627 (207) 348-6114

* **Jim Sharp,** motor vessel *Maine* (custom charter, water taxi service), 1 Sharp's Wharf, Camden, ME. (207) 236-9732 or (207) 236-9597.

*__The Eagle Island mailboat__ out of Sunset, ME., Robert Quinn (207) 348-2817. Take RT 15 into Deer Isle and turn right at the post office (marked with a "Sunset" sign), bear right again at Pressey Village Road (0.5mile), then left onto Dunham Point Road. Continue on to Sylvester Cove (about 3.2 miles from the post office)

*__To Isle au Haut__ (from Stonington, ME.)

  Mailboat/Ferry: *Miss Lizzie* makes scheduled trips to the town landing, about 0.8-1mile from the light; passengers going to the Keeper's House Bed & Breakfast are disembarked at the inn's private landing at Robinson Point. During the summer *The Mink* (June-Labor Day) takes visitors to Acadia National Park (Duck Harbor). *Miss Lizzie* daily June-September or by special arrangement. Isle au Haut Company, Herbert & George Aldrich (207) 367-5193 days, (207) 367-2355(evenings).

  The *Palmer Day* sails along the coastline of Isle au Haut for five miles. Palmer IV, P.O. Box 95, Stonington, ME. 04681 (207)-367-2207.

*__Schooner/windjammer cruises__ out of Camden, Rockport and Rockland
*__Maine State Ferry Service__, P.O. Box 645, Rockland, ME. 04841 (207) 596-2202

Air Charters:
* **Penobscot Air**, Knox Co. Airport, Owl's Head, ME. (207) 596-6211. (Just off RT 3 in Trenton)
* **Ace Aviation,** P.O. Box 457, Belfast, ME. (207)338-2970. (Just off Route 1 in Belfast-clearly marked)

 Penobscot Bay Area Lights:

* **Dick Moody, Offshore Freight & Passenger Co.**, Matinicus, ME. (207) 366-3700 (days), (207) 366-3926 (evenings). These trips are primarily birdwatching excursions to view the puffins and other seabirds at Matinicus Rock, but he will include good views of the lighthouse on request. Mid-June to mid-August, weekends only. Trips are made from Matinicus to Rockland during the week as needed and weather permitting; if planning to stay over on the island arrangements can be made to catch one of these boats.

* The *Betselma,* **Penobscot Bay Cruises** (Camden and Rockport Harbors), Camden Public Landing. (207) 236-2101.
* **Schooner/windjammer cruises** out of Camden, Rockport and Rockland
* **Jim Sharp,** motor vessel *Maine* (custom charter, water taxi service), 1 Sharp's Wharf, Camden, ME. (207) 236-9732 or (207) 236-9597.
* **Maine State Ferry Service**, P.O. Box 645, Rockland, ME. 04841 (207) 596-2202

Air Charters:
* **Penobscot Air,** Knox Co. Airport, Owl's Head, ME. (207) 596-6211. (RT 73 south from Rockland to Owl's Head- follow signs to airport)
* **Ace Aviation,** P.O. Box 457, Belfast, ME. (207)338-2970. (Just off Route 1 in Belfast-clearly marked)

Midcoast Lights:

Monhegan Island: Reached by boat from either Boothbay Harbor, New Harbor or Port Clyde:

Port Clyde:** From U.S. Route 1 in Thomaston, turn south onto ME 131 and follow this road through St. George and Tenant's Harbor into Port Clyde. The passenger ferry and mailboat from Port Clyde (Elizabeth Ann , Laura B***) provide service to the island year 'round. (207) 372-8848.

New Harbor:** From U.S. Route 1 in Waldoboro, take ME 32 to New Harbor. The ***Hardy III departs from Shaw's Fish & Lobster Wharf Restaurant. P.O. Box 326, New Harbor, ME. 04554 (207) 677-2026. Operates Memorial Day to mid-September

***Boothbay Harbor trips** (From US 1, take ME 27 south into Boothbay Harbor)
      -Capt. Fish's Boat Trips, Pier 1, (207) 633-3244 or (207) 633-2626
        Balmy Days Cruises, ***Balmy Days II***, Pier 8 P.O. Box 535, Boothbay Harbor, ME. 04538 (207) 633-2284. Operates mid-May to mid-October.

***Maine Maritime Museum** (Hardy Boat Co.) From US Route 1 in Bath, take the "Historic Bath" exit, turning onto Washington St. Follow the signs past Bath Iron Works to the Museum (clearly marked): 243 Washington St., Bath, ME. 04530 (207) 443-6100 or (207) 443-1316.

* The passenger ferry and/or mailboat to Monhegan from Pt. Clyde passes Marshall Point Light. (***Elizabeth Ann or Laura B***)
* **Jim Sharp,** motor vessel ***Maine,*** (custom charter, water taxi service), 1 Sharp's Wharf, Camden, ME. (207) 236-9732 or (207) 236-9597.

Air Charters:
* **Penobscot Air,** Knox Co. Airport, Owl's Head, ME. (207) 596-6211.
* **Ace Aviation,** P.O. Box 457, Belfast, ME. (207)338-2970.

 # Kennebec River & Boothbay Area Lights:

***Boothbay Harbor Trips** (From US 1, take ME 27 south into Boothbay Harbor)
      -Capt. Fish's Boat Trips, (207) 633-3244 or (207) 633-2626.
      -Balmy Days Cruises, P.O. Box 535. Boothbay Harbor, ME. 04538. (207) 633-2284.
***Maine Maritime Museum** (Hardy Boat Co)- 243 Washington St., Bath, ME. 04530 (207) 443-6100 or (207) 443-1316. From U.S. Route 1 in Bath, take the "Historic Bath" or "Front Street" exit, turning onto Washington St. Follow the signs past Bath Iron Works to the Museum (clearly marked): 243 Washington St., Bath, ME. 04530
***Boothbay Steamship Co.,** Landing Rd. Southport Island, ME. 04576, (207) 633-2500

 # Casco Bay & West Coast Lights:

***Jerry Sullivan** ("**The Happy Hooker**") specializes in charter fishing trips but will arrange a lighthouse trip which could include Pond Island, Halfway Rock, and others as far west as Cape Porpoise (Kennebunkport) as time and weather permit. P.O. Box 842, So. Harpswell, ME. 04079 (207) 833-5447

***Eagle Tours,** 19 Pilot Rd., Cape Elizabeth, ME. 04107 (207) 774-6498
***Bay View Cruises,** 184 Commercial St., Portland, ME. 04101 (207) 761-0496
***Longfellow Cruise Line**, One Long Wharf, Portland, ME. 04101 (207) 774-3578
***Casco Bay Lines,** P.O. Box 4656, Portland, ME. 04112 (207) 744-7871
Cape Arundel Cruises** (Elizabeth 2***), P.O. Box 840, Kennebunkport, ME. 04046 (207) 967-5595.

"**Isle of Shoals Steamship Co.,** Box 311 (315 Market St), Portsmouth, NH. 03802 1-800-441-4620. The sunset lighthouse cruise offers close views of Nubble, Whaleback and Portsmouth Harbor lights. These trips also go to the Isles of Shoals and White Island Light (NH).

Also:

It's often possible to find someone who will take you to an offshore lighthouse by asking around the fish pier at the nearest harbor; lobstermen are often willing after they've completed work. People I met were uniformly helpful and friendly.

The U.S. Lighthouse Society offers a tour of Maine lighthouses each fall, which includes lights from Portland Head to Penobscot Bay: *244 Kearney St., 5th Floor, San Francisco, CA. 94108, (415) 362-7255.*

The New England Lighthouse Foundation is a volunteer organization dedicated to the preservation and history of lighthouses and local lighthouse initiatives and organizations. *P.O. Box 1690, c/o Lighthouse Digest, Wells, ME . 04090.*

The Friends of Seguin is a group that works with restoration of the Seguin Island Light and the small museum in the keeper's house. The group also sponsors excursions to the island. *Friends of Seguin Island, P.O. Box 438, Georgetown, ME. 04548--* or contact the *Maine Maritime Museum in Bath, ME.* for additional information.

Friends of Acadia is a group working with the preservation and restoration of Baker Island Lighthouse. *P.O. Box 725, Bar Harbor, ME. 04609*

Friends of Nubble Light, a group working with restoration and maintenance of the Cape Neddick Lighthouse, *Box 9, c/o York Recreation and Parks Office, York, ME. 03909*

Marshall Point Lighthouse Museum, *P.O. Box 247, Port Clyde, ME. 04855.* Located in the keeper's house and recently restored kitchen building at Marshall Point Light. Open daily June through September (1-5pm), weekends during May and October.

The Fisherman's Museum (at Pemaquid Point Lighthouse); historical information and displays of the region's fishing and maritime industry. Owned by the Town of Bristol. *Pemaquid Point Rd., New Harbor, ME. 04554.* Open Memorial Day through Columbus Day.

Shore Village Museum: A comprehensive and impressive collection of lighthouse equipment, historical records and artifacts, including a variety of classical lenses, assembled by Ken Black. *104 Limerock St., Rockland, ME. 04841.* Open June to mid-October

LIGHTHOUSE	COLOR	CHARACTERISTICS	DESCRIPTION
East Quoddy Head	Red	Fixed	
Whitlock's Mill	Green	Equal 6 second intervals, light & dark	Height above water: 32 ft Range: 5nm
Mulholland (Inactive)	NA	NA	NA
West Quoddy Head	White	Group flashing white 15 seconds	Height above water: 83 ft Range: 18nm
Lubec Channel	White	Flashing 6 seconds	Height above water: 53 ft Range: 6nm
Little River (Inactive)	NA	NA	NA
Machias Seal Island	White	Flashing 3 seconds	Height above water: 82 ft Range:17 nm
Libby Island	White	Group flashing 20 seconds	Height above water: 91 ft Range:25 nm
Moose Peak	White	Flashing 30 seconds	Height above water: 72 ft Range: 26 nm
Nash Island (Inactive)	NA	NA	NA
Narraguagus (pond) Island (Inactive)	NA	NA	NA
Petit Manan Island	White	Flashing 10 seconds	Height above water: 123 ft Range: 26 nm
Prospect Harbor	Red with 2 white sectors	Flashing 6 seconds	Height above water: 42 ft Range: Red=7nm;white=9nm
Winter Harbor (Mark Island) (Inactive)	NA	NA	NA
Egg Rock	Red	Flashing 5 seconds	Height above water: 64 ft Range: 14 nm
Bear Island (Private Aid)	White	Flashing 5 seconds	Height above water:100 ft
Baker Island	White	Flashing 10 seconds	Height above water: 105 ft Range: 10 nm
Mt Desert Rock	White	Flashing 15 seconds	Height above water: 75 ft Range: 18 nm

LIGHTHOUSE	COLOR	CHARACTERISTIC	DESCRIPTION
Great Duck Island	Red	Flashing 5 seconds	Height above water: 67 ft Range: 19 nm
Bass Harbor Head	Red	Occulting 4 seconds	Height above water: 56 ft Range: 13 nm
Burnt Coat Harbor (Hockamock Head)	White	Occulting 4 seconds	Height above water: 75 ft Range: 9 nm
Blue Hill Bay (Inactive)	NA	NA	NA
Saddleback Ledge	White	Flashing 6 seconds	Height above water: 54 ft Range: 11nm
Isle au Haut	Red with white sector	Flashing 4 seconds	Height above water: 48 ft Range: Red=6nm;white=8nm
Eagle Island	White	Flashing 4 seconds	Height above water: 106 ft Range: 9nm
Mark Island (Deer Isle Thorofare)	White	Flashing 6 seconds	Height above water:52 ft Range: 8nm
Pumpkin Island (Inactive)	NA	NA	NA
Dice Head (Inactive)	NA	NA	NA
Fort Point (Stockton Springs)	White	Fixed	Height above water: 88 ft Range:15 nm
Grindle Point	Green	Flashing 4 seconds	Height above water: 39 ft Range: 6nm
Curtis Island	Green	Fixed	Height above water: 52 ft Range: 6 nm
Indian Island (Inactive)	NA	NA	NA
Goose Rocks	Red with white sector	Flashing red 6 seconds	Height above water: 51 ft Range: Red=11nm;white=12nm
Browns Head	White with 2 red sectors	Fixed	Height above water: 39 ft Range: Red=11nm;white=14nm
Rockland Breakwater	White	Flashing 5 seconds	Height above water: 39 ft Range: 17nm
Matinicus Rock	White	Flashing 10 seconds	Height above water: 90 ft Range: 20nm

LIGHTHOUSE	COLOR	CHARACTERISTIC	DESCRIPTION
Heron Neck	Red with white sector	Fixed	Height above water: 92 ft Range: Red=10nm;white=13nm
Two Bush Island	White with red sector	Flashing white 5 seconds	Height above water: 65 ft Range: Red=18nm;white=22nm
Rockland Harbor SW (Private aid)	Yellow	Flashing 2.5 seconds	Height above water: 35 ft
Owl's Head	White	Fixed	Height above water: 100 ft Range: 16 nm
Marshall Point	White	Fixed	Height above water: 30 ft Range: 13 nm
Whitehead Island	Green	Occulting 4 seconds	Height above water: 75 ft Range: 10 nm
Tenants Harbor (Inactive)NA	NA	NA	NA
Franklin Island	White	Flashing 6 seconds	Height above water: 57 ft Range: 8 nm
Pemaquid Point	White	Flashing 6 seconds	Height above water: 79 ft Range: 14 nm
Monhegan Island	White	Flashing 30 seconds	Height above water: 178 ft Range: 21nm
Ram Island	Red with 2 white sectors	Fixed	Height above water: 36ft Range: Red=9nm;white=11nm
Burnt Island	Red with 2 white sectors	Red flashing 6 seconds	Height above water: 61 ft Range:Red=12nm;white=15nm
Cuckholds	White	Group flashing twice every 6 seconds	Height above water: 59 ft Range: 12nm
Hendricks Head	White with red sector	Fixed	Height above water: 43 ft Range: Red=7nm;white=9nm
Seguin Island	White	Fixed	Height above water: 180 ft Range: 18nm
Pond Island	White	Equal 6 second intervals, light & dark	Height above water: 52 ft Range: 9nm
Perkins Island	Red with 2 white sectors	Flashing red 2.5 seconds	Height above water: 41ft Range: Red=5nm; white=6nm
Squirrel Point	Red with white sector	Equal interval red 6 seconds	Height above water: 25 ft Range: Red=7nm; white=9nm

LIGHTHOUSE	COLOR	CHARACTERISTIC	DESCRIPTION
Kennebec River Range Lights	Front=White Rear= White	Front=continuous quick flash Rear= Equal interval white 6 seconds	Height above water: Front=18 ft, Rear= 33 ft
Doubling Point	White	Flashing 4 seconds	Height above water: 23 ft Range: 9 nm
Halfway Rock	Red	Flashing 5 seconds	Height above water: 77 ft Range: 19 nm
Ram Island Ledge	White	Group flashing 6 seconds	Height above water: 77 ft Range: 12 nm
Portland Breakwater (Inactive)	NA	NA	NA
Spring Point Ledge	White with 3 red sectors	Flashing white 6 seconds	Height above water: 54 ft Range: Red=9nm;white=12nm
Portland Head	White	Flashing 4 seconds	Height above water: 101 ft Range: 24 nm
Cape Elizabeth (Two Lights)	White	Group flashing white (4 flashes) 15 seconds	Height above water: 129 ft Range: 15 nm
Wood Island	White & green	Alternating 10 seconds	Height above water: 71 ft Range: White=16nm; green=14nm
Goat Island	White	Flashing 6 seconds	Height above water: 38 ft Range: 12 nm
Cape Neddick (Nubble)	Red	Equal interval 6 seconds	Height above water: 88 ft Range: 13nm
Boon Island	White	Flashing white 5 seconds	Height above water: 137 ft Range: 19 nm
Whaleback	White	Group flashing twice every 10 seconds	Height above water: 59 ft Range: 24 nm
Portsmouth Harbor	Green	Fixed	Height above water: 52 ft Range: 12 nm

CatNap Publications
P.O. Box 172
Brunswick, Me. 04011